IMAGES
of America

ELBERT COUNTY

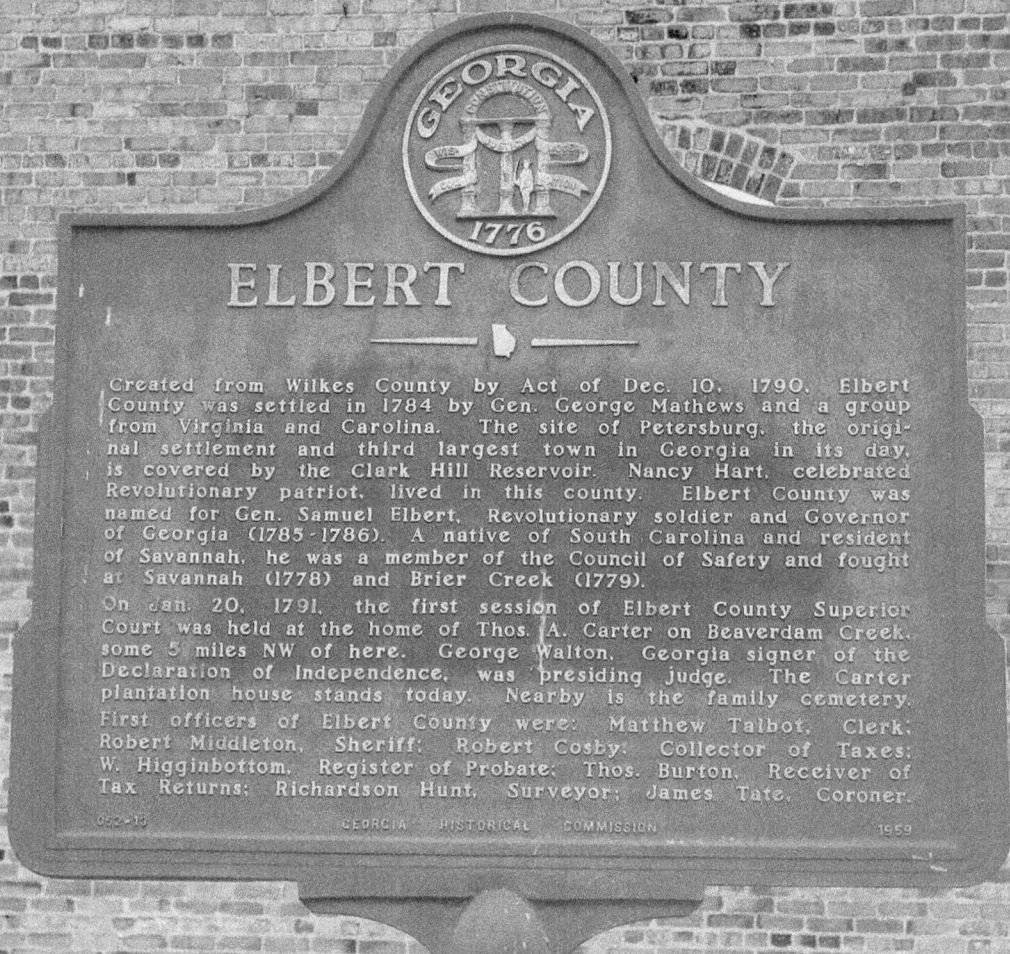

ELBERT COUNTY

Created from Wilkes County by Act of Dec. 10, 1790. Elbert County was settled in 1784 by Gen. George Mathews and a group from Virginia and Carolina. The site of Petersburg, the original settlement and third largest town in Georgia in its day, is covered by the Clark Hill Reservoir. Nancy Hart, celebrated Revolutionary patriot, lived in this county. Elbert County was named for Gen. Samuel Elbert, Revolutionary soldier and Governor of Georgia (1785-1786). A native of South Carolina and resident of Savannah, he was a member of the Council of Safety and fought at Savannah (1778) and Brier Creek (1779).

On Jan. 20, 1791, the first session of Elbert County Superior Court was held at the home of Thos. A. Carter on Beaverdam Creek, some 5 miles NW of here. George Walton, Georgia signer of the Declaration of Independence, was presiding judge. The Carter plantation house stands today. Nearby is the family cemetery.

First officers of Elbert County were: Matthew Talbot, Clerk; Robert Middleton, Sheriff; Robert Cosby, Collector of Taxes; W. Higginbottom, Register of Probate; Thos. Burton, Receiver of Tax Returns; Richardson Hunt, Surveyor; James Tate, Coroner.

052-13   GEORGIA   HISTORICAL   COMMISSION   1959

Elbert County has markers erected at important sites throughout its more than 300-square-mile geographic area. This marker stands to the north of the Elbert County Courthouse and contains important details about the history of the founding of the county. Visible in the background is the old Maxwell House Hotel, now home to Tena's Jewelry and Gifts and other shops. (Photograph by the author.)

ON THE COVER: In 1947, the driver education program at Elberton High School receives a new car from McLanahan Chevrolet Company. (Photograph by master photographer Everett Saggus; courtesy of Shirley and Walter McNeely.)

IMAGES
of America

ELBERT COUNTY

Joyce M. Davis

ARCADIA
PUBLISHING

Published by Arcadia Publishing
Charleston, South Carolina

Library of Congress Control Number: 2010932261

For all general information, please contact Arcadia Publishing:
Telephone 843-853-2070
Fax 843-853-0044
E-mail sales@arcadiapublishing.com
For customer service and orders:
Toll-Free 1-888-313-2665

Visit us on the Internet at www.arcadiapublishing.com

*To the memory of my mother, Maggie Marie
Wells Davis, who grew up in Heardmont*

CONTENTS

ACKNOWLEDGMENTS

For their photographic loans and other special assistance, I wish to thank the following individuals: Linda Aaron, Clyde Adams, Jean Adams, Gene Anderson, Iris Anderson, Stanley Ayers, Gene Bell, Jimmie Bell, Kim Black, James Blackstock, Danny Bridges, Phyllis Brooks, David Brown, Joan Brown, Lorene Godsey Brown, Sandra Brown, Jerome Cade, Rhonda Callaway, Pat Case, Tim Case, Gwen Childs, Martha Cole, Jane Coleman, Joyce Comolli, Rod Daniel, Carl Davis, Frances Davis, Jack W. Davis, Janice Dickerson, Tony Dickerson, Donna Lee Dixon, Beth Dunn, Ernie Dyal, Joane Dyal, Derek Dye, Shari Dye, Rebecca Eavenson, Val Evans, Frank Eaves, Bob Farmer III, Jane D. Farmer, Jimmy Farmer, Lynda Farmer, Carol Fernandez-Jones, Janet Floyd, Charlie Gaines, Imanell Gary, Ann Grace, Jimmy Hall, Glenna Hamilton, Tim Hamilton, Randy Haralson, Audrey Hardin, Horace Harper, Debbi Hartley, Sissie Herring, Clyde Hewell, Martha Hewell, Lat Heard, Linda Heard, Pat Jarvis, Steve Jenkins, Tom Jenkins, Bill Jones, Bobbie Jones, Gary Jones, Martha Lee Jones, Stockton Jones, Peggy Sue Kirkland, Glenn Kowalski, Mary Dana Leverett, Rob Leverett, Mary Palmer Linnemann, Jane Godsey Lunceford, Martha Lutz, Bunnie Lyle, Stuart Lyle, Jack McConnell, Jenny McConnell, Shirley McNeely, Walter McNeely, Carolyn Miller, Laverne Mills, Nelson Morgan, Josephine Oglesby, Tom Oglesby, Tina Poole, Kerri Pruitt, Pat Rathbone, Tom Robinson, Earl Saxon, Shane Scoggins, Scottie Scultz, Juanita Seigler, Judy Seigler, Susan Sexton, Nancy Seymour, Barbara Slay, Marilyn Slocombe, Larry Smith, Pam Smith, Jackie Dickerson Thompson, Lavonia Dickerson Turner, Melinda Turner, Otis Vickery, Chuck Waters, Carol Webb, Chester Webb, Darlene West, Daryl West, Ronnie West, Richard Elbert Whitehead, Darla Wilson, Larry Wilson, and Tracie York. If I have omitted a name, I am sorry for the omission.

Also, I found the staffs of the following institutions very helpful: Elberton Granite Association, Inc.; the *Elberton Star*; Elbert County Chamber of Commerce; Elbert County Historical Society; Elbert County Library; Elbert County Sheriff's Office, Lake Arrowhead Point Golf Course; Love Unlimited; Tena's Jewelry and Gifts; and U. S. Army Corps of Engineers.

I also wish to thank my Arcadia editors, Katie Shayda and Brinkley Taliaferro, for their great assistance and enduring patience throughout this book production.

INTRODUCTION

Elbert County is located in northeast Georgia and is bordered on the east by the Savannah River and on the south and west by the Broad River. It is surrounded by Lincoln, Wilkes, and Oglethorpe Counties to the south, Madison and Franklin Counties to the west, and Hart County to the north. After the settlement of Georgia in 1733, sections of the large area of the state that became Elbert County were settled by the mid- to late 18th century; but the formal beginning of Elbert County occurred in 1790, when a sizable portion of territory in northeastern Georgia was separated from the large county of Wilkes and turned into a new county named in honor of Samuel Elbert (1740–1788), Mason, merchant, son of a Baptist minister, hero of the American Revolution, and governor of Georgia from 1785 to 1786, when the University of Georgia was chartered (1785). At the time, the state honored each new county by bestowing upon it the name of a recently deceased important Georgian. In this case, former governor Samuel Elbert had died two years earlier.

Much of the early history of the territory that became Elbert County was tied to the presence of the Savannah and Broad Rivers, which frame the area on the east, south and west and meet in the southeastern part of the county, at what was known then as the Point. There, Gov. James Wright built Fort James, where settlers from Virginia, North Carolina, and South Carolina entered Georgia and registered as new residents. In the early years, food gathering was critical to survival, and fishing on the rivers provided one source of food. Trapping and hunting were also activities essential to putting meals on early settlers' tables. Later as the patriotic movement in the 13 colonies heated up and expanded into resistance to British control, the rivers continued to play a vital role in the lives of the settlers by providing both opportunities and obstacles to heroic action, as the river crossings figured in a number of key battles. A number of decisive victories for the American cause both began and ended in the area that would become Elbert County or took place near its borders. Dominating the list of heroic leaders of the American Revolution in the land that became Elbert County were Nancy Hart, a pioneer woman who spied on and killed British soldiers for the American cause; Stephen Heard, a future Georgia governor who figured in major battles; Barnard Heard, brother of Stephen Heard; and Dan Tucker, on whose life a famous folk tune was reputedly based.

Following the Revolution and the establishment of Elbert County, towns began to be formed. Dartmouth was an early fortified establishment at Fort James and soon yielded to Petersburg, which began as a tobacco warehouse and evolved into one of the most important cities in the state as its prosperity expanded almost exponentially with the construction of tobacco warehouses. With the waning of the tobacco industry and the introduction of cotton farming, as well as the attendant problems of poor means of shipping cotton by land from Petersburg, other towns in Elbert County began to eclipse Petersburg in importance. These included Ruckersville, which was named after Ruckersville, Virginia, and Heardmont, a settlement named after the large manor house of Stephen Heard, a hero of the American Revolution and Georgia governor in

1780–1781. The small towns of Middleton, Dewy Rose, and Bowman were established at about the same time. Most important of all these towns, however, was Elberton, the county seat. The name Elberton came to be used for the town after Elbertville and others had been tried, and the city of Elberton was incorporated in 1803. The first session of Elbert County court was held soon after the creation of the county in a makeshift courthouse on the plantation of Revolutionary Thomas A. Carter. Despite the informality of the venue, however, these court actions held in the private home bore the same authority and resonance as decisions made in the formal courthouses that would follow. Soon after the first court session, an early courthouse was constructed, and in the early 19th century, a second courthouse was built in the middle of what is now named Sutton Square, the central public square in the city. In the early 1890s, following a well-orchestrated public appeal to the citizens of Elbert County through a series of newspaper articles, the county chose to build a new courthouse. This third and present courthouse was designed by native architect Reuben Harrison Hunt, and after a number of repairs, both major and minor, remains in use for the citizens of Elbert County.

Cotton became a dominant crop in Elbert County during the late 19th century, primarily as a result of development of the cotton gin and improvements in the means of bringing a viable cotton product to market; and it led to the growth of the cotton industry, which required warehouses for storage and sale, buyers for the cotton crop, and the means to deliver the product to the buyers and ultimately to larger markets outside the county and state. The development of the railroad industry and the introduction of rail lines into Elbert County, in 1878, with the construction of the Elberton Air Line Railroad that ran from Elberton to Toccoa, Georgia, provided the small towns of the county access to large cities and faraway destinations. Travel into and out of Elbert County up to that time had been by stagecoach, on the old post road from Elberton to Lexington, Georgia, now indicated by a Georgia Historical Society marker. Trains provided a means to take Elbertonians to distant places and to bring passengers to Elberton for shopping in the growing mercantile district. They also served for commercial transport, as much of the cotton grown in Elbert County went to large markets elsewhere on trains.

A third major industry arose in the late 19th century in Elbert County and grew to dominate all other industries in the town and the entire county. In the last quarter of the 19th century, the presence of an especially pure strain of blue granite was found in large veins beneath the soil in the county. As quarrying for the granite began to develop, sheds were built for carving this product into monuments, statues, architectural ornaments, and architectural structural elements, to name many of its uses. The industry began to grow and have regional, state, national, and, ultimately, international importance. By the mid-20th century, the city of Elberton was well known as the "Granite Capital of the World." Granite markers used as welcome signs throughout the county demonstrate to visitors the importance and prevalence of the granite industry in Elberton and Elbert County and, at the same time, define the region as "granite country."

Educational facilities in Elbert County appeared early in the form of academies, and there were quite a number established in the early 19th century. Tutors also taught children of well-to-do citizens, and regional schools were established throughout the county following the Civil War. Modern developments have consisted of consolidating area schools and making school systems free and public. Finally, racial integration was achieved in the county by 1970. Sports, recreation, industry, travel, religion, service, culture, politics, and learning have been components as well of life in Elbert County, as lived by its citizens for more than two centuries. Historical celebration also has captured the imagination of the county's leaders; in 1990, the county marked its bicentennial with a year of special newspaper articles, historical events, costume celebrations, and historical recordings, including the burial of a special time capsule.

Elbert County, both in name and deed, honors the memory of the American patriot Samuel Elbert; the persona of this early patriot survives in stories told about him on many historic occasions taking place in the city of Elberton or the county of Elbert and in the form of a monument dedicated to him in 1992.

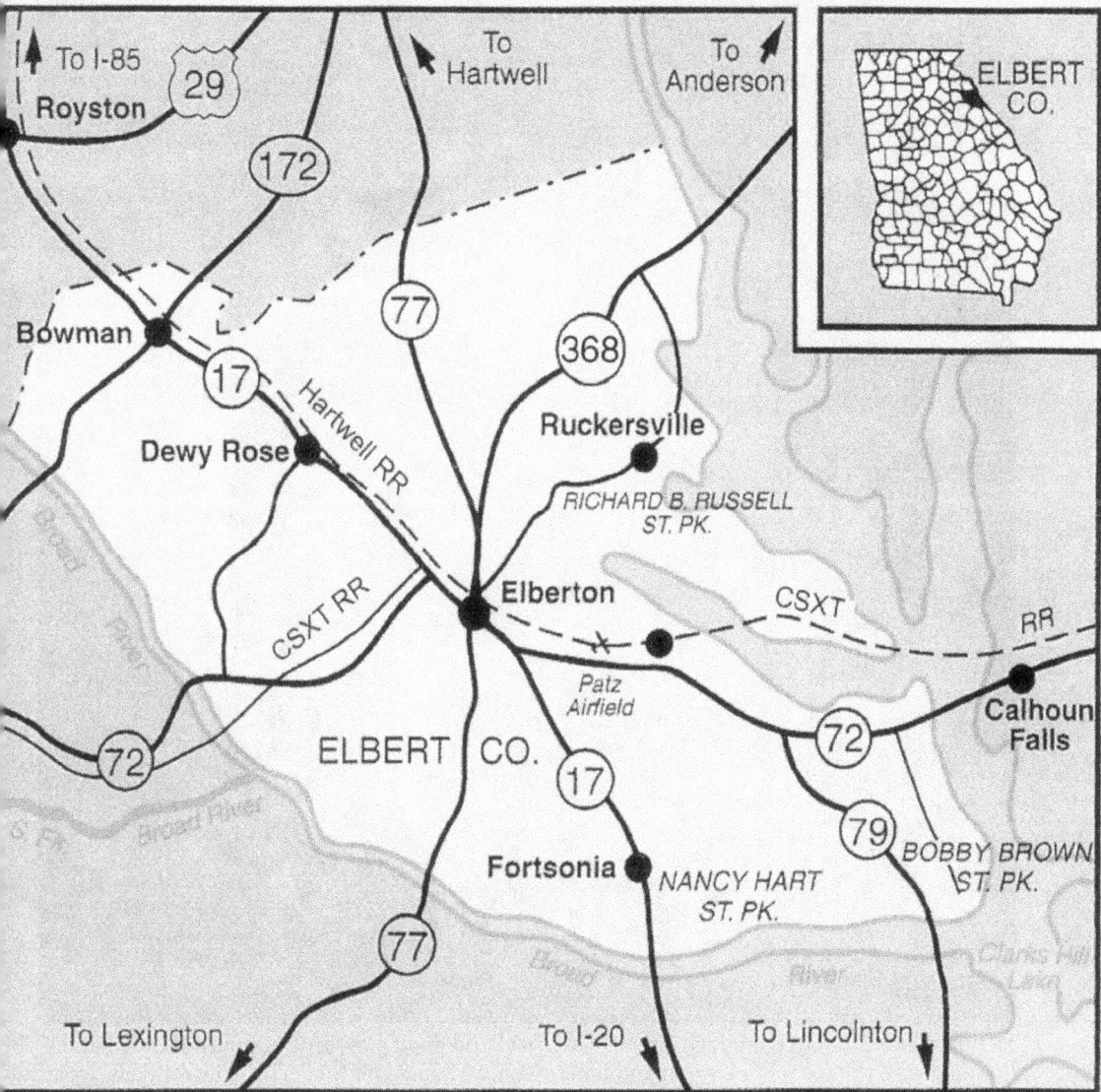

This map of Elbert County, Georgia, illustrates the vastness of the geographical area covered by Elbert County and the close proximity of the Savannah and Broad Rivers to historical sites spread throughout the county.

Samuel Elbert displayed courage on the battlefield and good judgment in political office and is honored with the town of Elberton and Elbert County named for him. This image, taken from a locket owned by Richard Elbert Whitehead, a direct descendant, is the primary surviving image of Elbert and has been used to illustrate articles and for other references to this great patriot of the American Revolution. (Courtesy of Richard Elbert Whitehead.)

One

Elbert County Monuments

Elbert County was established December 10, 1790, by the Georgia General Assembly and named in honor of Samuel Elbert, a former Georgia governor and Revolutionary War hero who had deceased a few years prior. The committee charged with selecting a site for the seat of this new county included Stephen Heard, another former Georgia governor and war hero. They chose a small settlement formed in 1769, according to legend cited by Janelle Jones McRee, one of the premier historians of Elbert County, in *The Elbert County Bicentennial Commemorative Historical Book*. McRee writes that William Woodley's family and a few others stopped at a spot in what would become Elberton, at a spring located in a ravine, and that the group of weary travelers found the water from the spring so invigorating that they chose to settle in the area, naming the site Old Town Springs. Woodley and his family then built a house on the hill overlooking the spring. In the mid-20th century, the Stephen Heard chapter of the Daughters of the American Revolution (DAR) placed a marker on the site of this first known dwelling in the town of Elberton.

The first court session in the new county was held on the premises of the Thomas A. Carter plantation, with court being held inside the Carter house. Soon afterward, the first courthouse was constructed. John H. McIntosh, official historian of Elbert County and author of *History of Elbert County, Georgia, 1790–1935*, locates that first courthouse somewhere behind the present one, on the western side of the square. This would have placed it close to the ravine with the miraculous springs that drew Woodley and other settlers. McIntosh also speculates that the first permanent courthouse was constructed of logs.

Initially the new county seat was called Elbertville, incorporating the name of Samuel Elbert, but was changed to Elbert County Court House, according to McRee. Finally, in 1803, the village was incorporated with the name Elberton, even though there was another town of the same name (also named for Samuel Elbert) in Effingham County, near Savannah, which had ceased to thrive by 1803. The seat of Elbert County in northeast Georgia, however, endured.

A second constructed courthouse for Elbert County, built in the center of the public square and mandated by an act of the Georgia Assembly, stood until 1893, when calls for a new building to replace it led to construction of the present courthouse, built in 1894 and opened for business at the beginning of 1895. The Elbert County Courthouse is one of many historical structures in a county filled with markers and monuments dedicated to the heroic deeds of its creators and is the starting point for any tour of this county that is more than two centuries old.

The third permanent Elbert County Courthouse was built in 1894 and inaugurated at the beginning of January 1895. Architect Reuben Harrison Hunt employed the popular Richardsonian Romanesque style and practice of combining brick and granite for the exterior, with only a small amount of wood on the outside, to save on future repairs. His grand building is still in use today, following extensive renovation from 2005 to 2008 under the direction of Dennis Young, head of the county's construction department. Although many county offices are now located in the Elbert County Complex on College Avenue, offices on the main level of the courthouse are filled; current plans provide for the reopening, at some point, of the courtroom on the second floor. This present courthouse replaced the early-19th-century second courthouse, located in the center of the public square, which, in turn, had replaced the first courthouse built in the late 18th century, possibly of logs. (Courtesy of the *Elberton Star*.)

In May 1893, Elbert County native Reuben Harrison Hunt returned to Elberton from his successful architectural practice in Chattanooga, Tennessee, to present his plan for a new courthouse to the Elbert County Board of Commissioners. His proposal was accepted, and a grand building that will stand the test of time was constructed. On the day of the building's opening, Hunt praised his contractor and workers, as well as Elbert County commission chairman E. B. Tate, for the good work on the building and for making the grand edifice possible. (Courtesy of the Elbert County Historical Society.)

More than two centuries elapsed in Elbert County before there was a monument within its boundaries to honor Samuel Elbert. In 1991, William A. Kelly, retired executive vice president of the Elberton Granite Association, Inc. (EGA), presented a program about Elbert to the Elbert County Historical Society, in which he noted the absence of a Samuel Elbert marker. Kelly's speech led to action by members of the EGA. Willie Simmons, owner of Sweet City Quarries, Inc., donated a block of royal blue granite, finished by Supreme Granite Company, Inc.; Ed Mims designed the monument; Anne Jenson etched an image of Elbert, based on a miniature portrait of Elbert owned by his direct descendant Richard Elbert Whitehead; and Tom Oglesby's Keystone Memorials, Inc., provided the letterings on the monument, which was erected October 27, 1992, on the western side of the Elbert County Historical Society Meetinghouse, the restored 1910 Seaboard Air Line Depot. (Photograph by the author.)

Dated 1969 by the DAR, the first recorded dwelling in Elberton overlooked the springs where William Woodley and his family stopped to drink water and settle, naming the spot Old Town Springs. In November 1961, the site was marked with a now-lost plaque by Mabel Mann (left), regent, and Annie Lee Stovall (right), historian, of the Stephen Heard chapter of the DAR. (Courtesy of the *Elberton Star*.)

Transportation to Elberton and communication with the outside world have improved significantly since the early days of travel by stagecoach over rough roads. Post riders carried mail over this road, indicated by a Georgia Historical Society marker installed in 1955, in front of the Elbert County Courthouse. (Photograph by the author.)

The Elbert County Courthouse forms a backdrop for a modern memorial. In 1976, the city and county, with the assistance of Turner Concrete Company and the Elberton-Elbert County Bicentennial Committee, erected the American Bicentennial Eagle monument on the western side of the square. The Elbert County Courthouse, which stands proudly behind it, has since been revitalized by a major renovation project, which included the repainting of the building red to cover a gray coat added in the mid-20th century. (Photograph by the author.)

Two

Revolutionary Activity

The land that became Elbert County was filled with early American patriots who battled fierce odds by living in a large territory ceded earlier by Native Americans, with two rivers providing sustenance and transportation. The rivers later played a part in the war itself. In the American Revolutionary Battle of Cherokee Ford, February 11, 1779, a small band of American patriots met British commander Colonel Boyd in a skirmish at the place on the Savannah River that was the major passage from Georgia to South Carolina. This spot was a part of what was then Wilkes County but would become Elbert County after its creation in 1790. A short fight left British commander Colonel Boyd with heavy losses, including 100 dead and wounded in his force of approximately 800 troops. Many were volunteers, however; John H. McIntosh notes that a number of Boyd's men deserted and went over to the American Patriot side.

The notable impact of this Pyrrhic victory for Boyd was the weakening of his troop level, which quite likely determined the outcome of a major battle he fought against the Americans a few days after this skirmish. McIntosh asserted that the Battle of Kettle Creek, three days later on February 14, 1779, was decisive for the success of the American side in the northern Georgia region.

The Battle of Kettle Creek, which took place on a site that remained part of Wilkes County after the creation of Elbert County, left the British commander Colonel Boyd fatally wounded. Significant also is that this battle stopped Boyd's planned march northward to Washington, Georgia. Major Spurgen replaced Boyd, who was dying and able only to look on passively as his side lost the battle, despite the numerical superiority of the British side. McIntosh notes that the American colonel Pickens went to Boyd after the heat of battle subsided and offered final service to the fallen British colonel. Boyd asked Capt. Hugh McCall, who was with Pickens, to let him have water and someone to bury him after he died. Boyd also dictated a letter for his wife and turned over articles the American commanders promised to send to her. Boyd died early in the evening of the day of the big loss at Kettle Creek.

McIntosh, writing in 1935, expressed chagrin that the Battle of Kettle Creek had not received full recognition for its significance. He stressed that the battle forced British commander Colonel Campbell to abandon the Augusta area and retreat to Savannah, leaving behind ammunition that aided the American Revolutionaries. The battle has since become recognized for its significance.

Interest in Elbert County history and the American Revolution has enabled many citizens and special interest groups to become enlightened about the lives of these early American heroes who played prominent roles in the creation of Elbert County.

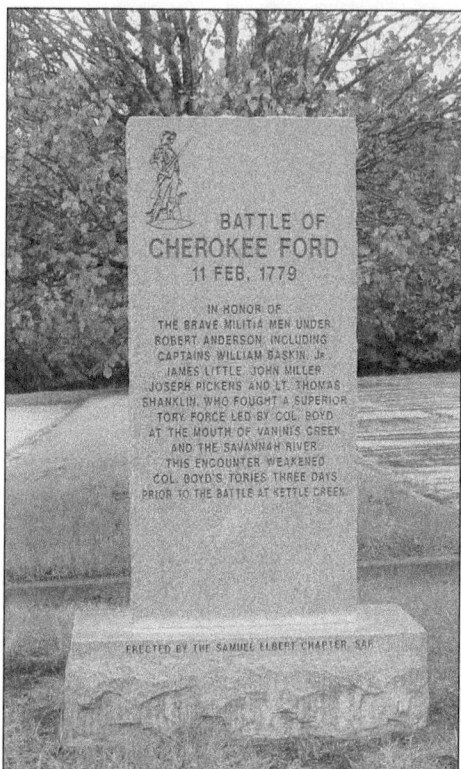

The Samuel Elbert chapter of Sons of the American Revolution erected a granite marker at Richard B. Russell State Park to celebrate the skirmish at Cherokee Ford, near Van's Creek, on February 11, 1779. Though this battle was lost by the American patriots, heavy British casualties assured American success in the next battle, on February 14, at Kettle Creek in Wilkes County, which stopped the northward progress of the British. (Photograph by the author.)

The Point is a site where the Savannah and Broad Rivers converge in the southeastern part of Elbert County. Here early colonists from three states crossed into Georgia and were registered at Fort James, for which Governor Wright authorized construction. The site is identified by this Georgia Historical Society marker just off Highway 72 East, on the road leading to the specific location, 8 miles to the southeast. (Photograph by the author.)

Stephen Heard (1740–1815), illustrated on Silverheels, moved from Virginia to Wilkes County, Georgia, in the mid-18th century and participated in the Battle of Kettle Creek. Taken prisoner later, he escaped being hanged for treason in Augusta when a female slave named Mammy Kate transported him out of jail in a large basket, on the ruse of doing his laundry. (Courtesy of Hargrett Rare Book and Manuscript Library/University of Georgia Libraries.)

Stephen Heard is buried in the private family cemetery in Heardmont. Elected to the Georgia Assembly, he was appointed governor (1780–1781) to replace George Wells, who was killed in a duel, and in 1803 was one of three committee members chosen to select a county seat. With nearly 7,000 acres in postwar grants, Heard built Heardmont, a palatial home that gave its name to the small community that grew up around it. (Photograph by the author.)

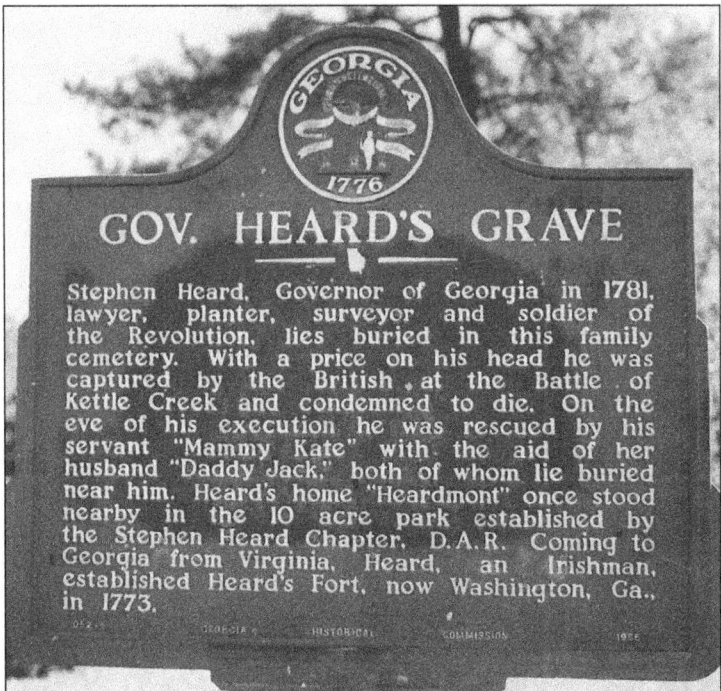

GEORGIA 1776

GOV. HEARD'S GRAVE

Stephen Heard, Governor of Georgia in 1781, lawyer, planter, surveyor and soldier of the Revolution, lies buried in this family cemetery. With a price on his head he was captured by the British at the Battle of Kettle Creek and condemned to die. On the eve of his execution he was rescued by his servant "Mammy Kate" with the aid of her husband "Daddy Jack," both of whom lie buried near him. Heard's home "Heardmont" once stood nearby in the 10 acre park established by the Stephen Heard Chapter, D.A.R. Coming to Georgia from Virginia, Heard, an Irishman, established Heard's Fort, now Washington, Ga., in 1773.

During the Revolutionary War, Nancy Ann Morgan Hart (c. 1735–1830), shown in a photographic reproduction of an early artistic image made when she was about 25 to 30, spied for the American patriots, killed British soldiers, and possibly participated in combat at Kerttle Creek on February 14, 1779. A few years before the Revolution began, Hart moved with her family into the southeast portion of what would become Elbert County and reflected personal valor and fearlessness during the struggle for American independence. (Courtesy of the *Elberton Star*.)

The Georgia Historical Society marker on Highway 17 South indicates the road leading to the Nancy Hart Park, featuring a replica of her cabin. Her story has survived in both her descendants' accounts and in scholarly research. Irene Wilcox, quoting Edna Arnold Copeland, an Elberton authority on Hart, dispels many of the anecdotal clichés, including one that she was cross-eyed. (Photograph by the author.)

NANCY HART
←——— 1½ mi. ———→

On Wahatche (War Woman) Creek, in Revolutionary times, lived Nancy Morgan Hart, her husband, Benjamin, and their children. Six feet tall, masculine in strength and courage, Nancy Hart was a staunch patriot, a deadly shot, a skilled doctor, and a good neighbor. A spy for the colonists, she is credited with capturing several Tories. Later, with her son, John, and his family, she joined a wagon train to Henderson County, Kentucky, where she is buried. Hart County, the Nancy Hart Highway, and schools in Elbert and Hart Counties are named for her. A replica of her log home, with chimney stones from the original, is in the Nancy Hart Park, 1½ miles from here.

A replica of Nancy Hart's log cabin in southeastern Elbert County, near the Broad River, is at the site where Hart proved her resilience as a frontier resident able to handle guns and act quickly in dangerous situations. John H. McIntosh cites an incident from Elizabeth Ellet's *Women of the Revolution*, in which Hart held a small contingent of British soldiers at bay by plying them with food and drink and slyly taking their weapons while her daughter went out to signal for help. When one drunken Tory arose to defend himself, Hart shot him dead and wounded another, guarding the rest until her husband arrived with help. Hart scholar Edna Arnold Copeland notes that the cabin replica was rebuilt around the original fireplace. (Photograph by master photographer Everett Saggus; courtesy of the Elbert County Historical Society.)

John Darden Jr. was a captain in the North Carolina militia and a Revolutionary soldier. His niece Elizabeth Darden, the daughter of his brother George, married Stephen Heard. Darden is buried in the Heard family cemetery at Heardmont. (Photograph by the author.)

The Reverend Daniel Tucker (1740–1818), a Revolutionary soldier sometimes connected to the folk song "Old Dan Tucker," came to the territory from Virginia and, in 1798, bought Cook's Ferry Tract from John Heard. In 1817, the Georgia legislature allowed him to run a public ferry on the Savannah River. Tucker died in early April 1818, three days after writing his will. (Photograph by the author.)

Three

County Creation
and Growth

Several early towns were established in the territory before Elbert County was created. Some of these towns faded away, leaving only a few artifacts behind, while others remain as mere remnants of themselves. A large portion of land in the eastern part of the county has been inundated by waters impounded by one of several dams built on the Savannah River. Dartmouth, in the fork of the Savannah and Broad Rivers, was a fortress and the first real settlement in the territory that became Elbert County. John H. McIntosh says the unknown population of that community was large enough for a stockade named Fort James. Dartmouth was an active community with approximately 300 residents in 1773–1775, a period for which McIntosh cites land court records. It later gave way to the more prosperous Petersburg. Ellis Merton Coulter's *Old Petersburg and the Broad River Valley of Georgia*, a definitive study of Petersburg, is another source for the story of its development.

In 1784, Gen. George Mathews of Virginia led a large contingent of Virginia and North Carolina residents to a site in what was then Wilkes County. In 1786, the Georgia General Assembly authorized Dionysius Oliver to erect a tobacco warehouse on his land. Because the recently settled Virginia and North Carolina tobacco farmers found the soil conducive to tobacco growth and stored their harvests in Oliver's warehouse until it could be shipped, this warehouse became the core of the new town, named for his native Petersburg, Virginia. More warehouses were built, and other commercial sites appeared quickly, leading to rapid community growth and a population of 2,000 served by a commission government, a social club, and two U.S. senators serving simultaneously—William W. Bibb and Charles Tait.

Cotton followed tobacco as the dominant crop, and warehousing the two became big business. Shipping these products to market, with flatboats bringing needed supplies back, became difficult and unreliable because of varying river levels. Because land transport was extremely difficult, dependency on the river for shipment of Petersburg's products no doubt led to the demise of the town, the fourth largest and one of the most important cities in Georgia in the early 19th century. By the early 1820s, though, the town was on the wane; by 1830, the end was in sight for this magical city of the past. Other major early towns in future Elbert County territory included Ruckersville, settled in 1773 by aristocrats from Virginia, who named it after the town of Ruckersville, Virginia, and incorporated it in 1822; and Heardmont, named for Heard's manor house. The growth of Heardmont continued in the period leading up to the Civil War and faded in the early 20th century, with the failures of cotton and the rerouting of automobile traffic to the south of the Heardmont-to-Elberton railroad route. Academies were mandated by the state legislature and played prominent roles in the lives of these communities, and large estate homes became part of the spreading settlement.

In the late 18th century, prominent settlers in Elbert County included the Allen brothers from Virginia, who became merchants over a wide area extending as far as South Carolina. William built a house between 1784 and 1790, with additions, including the front portico, made later. In 1933, William Etsel Snowden Jr. referred to it as the oldest extant house in Elbert County; but, after its long survival, the house burned in the early 21st century. (Courtesy of the *Elberton Star*.)

The Alexander-Cleveland house, dated about 1741, which stood on the hill where Coldwater Creek empties into the Savannah River, was said to be the oldest house in Elbert County, with many of its timbers cut from trees in the area near the house. This residence, which was on the National Register of Historic Places, burned in 1982. (Courtesy of the *Elberton Star*.)

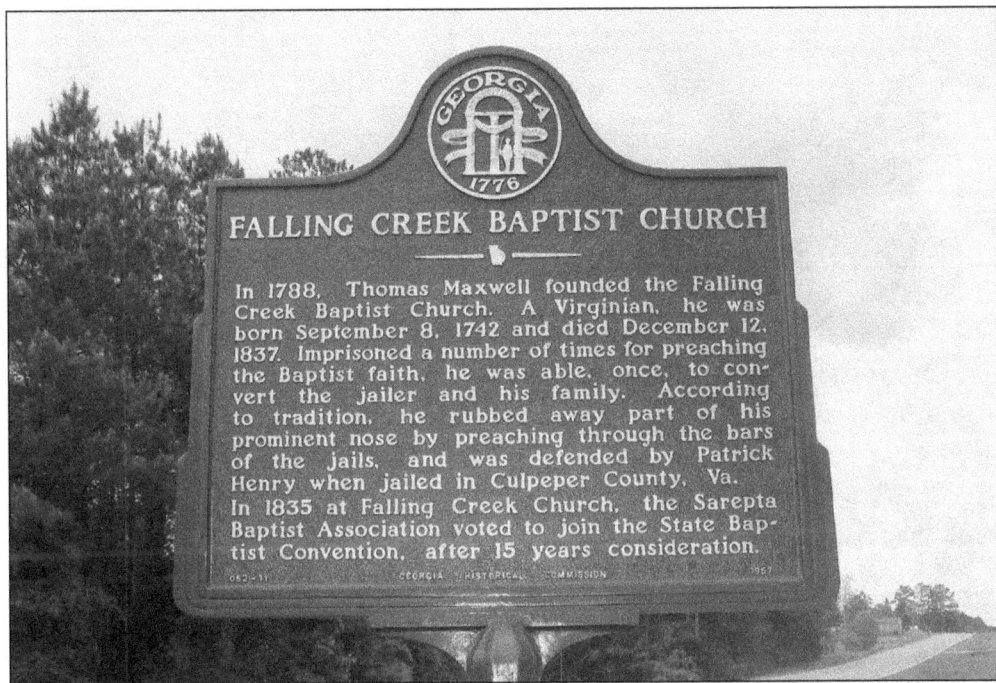

FALLING CREEK BAPTIST CHURCH

In 1788, Thomas Maxwell founded the Falling Creek Baptist Church. A Virginian, he was born September 8, 1742 and died December 12, 1837. Imprisoned a number of times for preaching the Baptist faith, he was able, once, to convert the jailer and his family. According to tradition, he rubbed away part of his prominent nose by preaching through the bars of the jails, and was defended by Patrick Henry when jailed in Culpeper County, Va.
In 1835 at Falling Creek Church, the Sarepta Baptist Association voted to join the State Baptist Convention, after 15 years consideration.

One of the Georgia Historical Society markers placed in Elbert County is located at the Falling Creek Baptist Church, which was founded in 1788, by the Reverend Thomas Maxwell, a Baptist preacher from Virginia. (Photograph by the author.)

Rose Hill, the home built before 1832 by Elizabeth Darden Heard for her son Thomas Jefferson Heard, was later the site of the Seaboard Air Line Traveling Library (organized 1898), which Sally Harper Heard began after the death of her son. Rose Hill remained in the Heard family until May 1946, when Mamie Latimer Heard sold it to W. C. Johnson of Miami and returned to the Heard family home on Heard Street. Like many other venerable houses in Elbert County, however, Rose Hill did not survive. It burned in 1964, under the ownership of Ross L. Brown, who bought it in 1961. (Courtesy of Lat and Linda Heard.)

The Singleton Allen house, shown in a sketch published in 1933 by William Etsel Snowden Jr., was built in 1845 in the southeastern part of Elbert County. By the 20th century, it had become the home of Earle McCalla. Early visitors to the house described its once elegant interior furnishings. At some point in the late 20th century, the house was demolished. (Courtesy of the author.)

Van's Creek Baptist Church in Ruckersville, near the site of a February 1779 Revolutionary War skirmish, was founded by the Reverend Dozier Thornton of Virginia. The spot was named after David Van, a Cherokee chief converted to Christianity by Thornton. The building, site of the Georgia Baptist Convention of 1837, is seen here in a photograph before it was covered with a brick veneer in 1953. (Courtesy of the *Elberton Star*.)

This house on Old Petersburg Road was said to be a wedding present for Asa and Lauriette Hamilton Chandler and was built in the early 19th century near Falling Creek Baptist Church, where Chandler was preaching at the time. In 1917, Walter C. Jones, father of historians Neva Jones and Janelle Jones McRee, purchased the home because its features were characteristic of antebellum farmhouses. The house was placed on the National Register of Historic Places in 1982. (Photograph by the author.)

The Ruckersville Methodist Church, in northeastern Elbert County, was built in 1832 on land donated by Peter Alexander. Trustees Richard Adams, Alfred Hammond, and John Jones and their successors were given authority to employ a marshal with sheriff's powers in a 3-mile area, a power that still stands. The exterior still has its original wooden siding. A granite marker sits on bricks taken from the original church building. (Photograph by the author.)

Stinchcomb Methodist Church, more than a century old, is one of the oldest churches in continuous use in Elbert County. Notable burial markers in the cemetery of the Stinchcomb United Methodist Church graveyard include those of a number of Revolutionary and Civil War veterans. (Photograph by the author.)

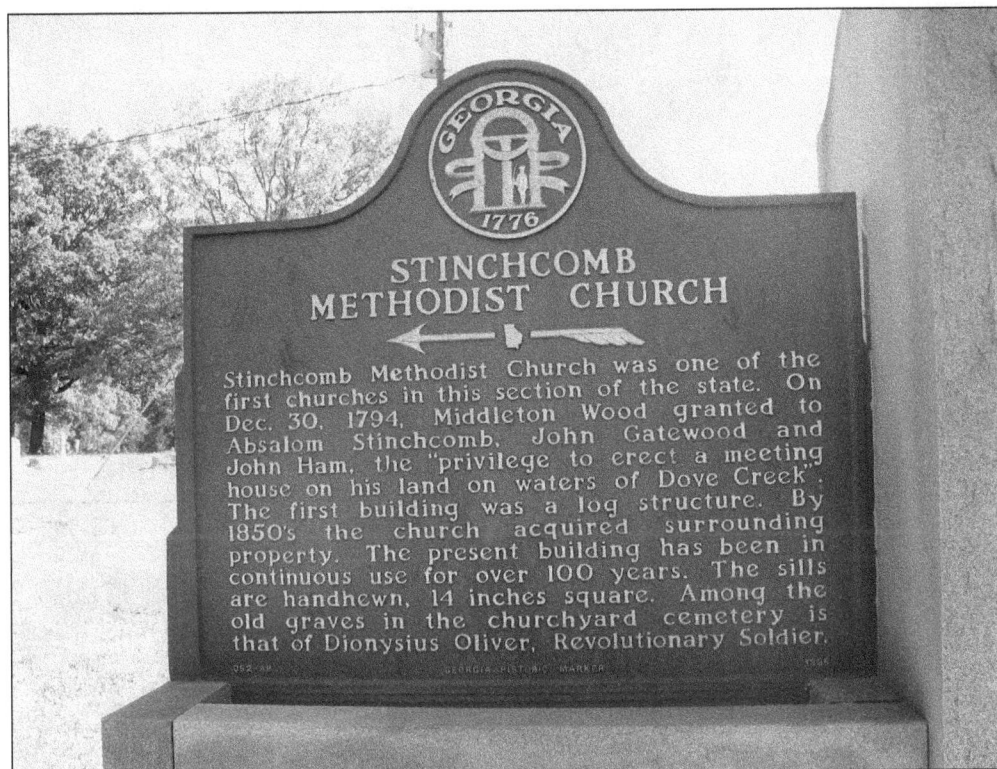

A Georgia Historical Society marker at Stinchcomb Methodist Church reveals the history of this old church. (Photograph by the author.)

Bethlehem Methodist Church, on the Calhoun Falls Highway (Georgia 72 East), was established in 1787 at a building about 2 miles away and named Thompson's Meeting House. Cited as the "oldest active Methodist Church and the oldest continuing congregation in Georgia Methodism" on a plaque on its present facade, the wooden frame building shown here was constructed in 1803–1804 and replaced in 1959 by a brick building. (Courtesy of the *Elberton Star*.)

Ralph Banks, a captain in the Revolutionary War, came to the Elbert County area from Virginia and built a house in the Coldwater Creek area, in the northeastern part of the county. Dated as early as the 1780s or as late as around 1800, it was placed on the National Register of Historic Places in 1978 and is believed to be the site of a number of important early Methodist church conferences. (Photograph by the author.)

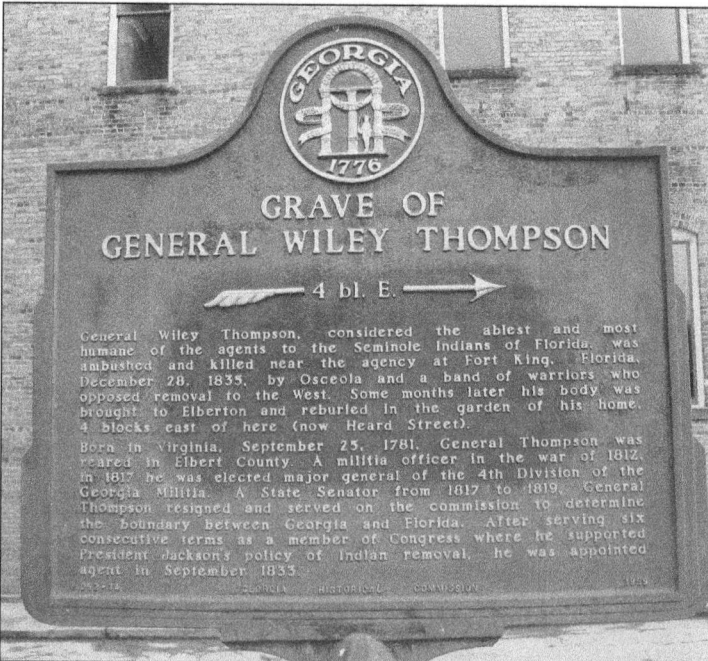

Gen. Wiley Thompson, a native Virginian who grew up in Elberton and served as a War of 1812 militia officer and state senator from 1817 to 1819, died in Florida in 1835, killed by Seminole chief Osceola. Wiley's body was reburied in Elberton, in his garden on Heard Street, and moved again, in 1960, to the new Forest Hills Memorial Park on Highway 77 South. This marker is located in front of the Elbert County Courthouse. (Photograph by the author.)

Identified as the Moses Fleming home by Janelle Jones McRee, this 19th-century house on South McIntosh Street was later in the Adams family for four generations. (Photograph by the author.)

This cabin, originally the kitchen of the Frances and Winslow Rowzee home on Gregg Shoals, came into ownership of Josephine Oglesby's father. Rowzee, who represented Elbert County as a lieutenant in the War of 1812, was one of many transplanted Virginians living in Elbert County. Oglesby moved the cabin to her backyard on Hartwell Highway and has had it open for events, including the Georgia Trust Ramble in 2007. (Photograph by the author.)

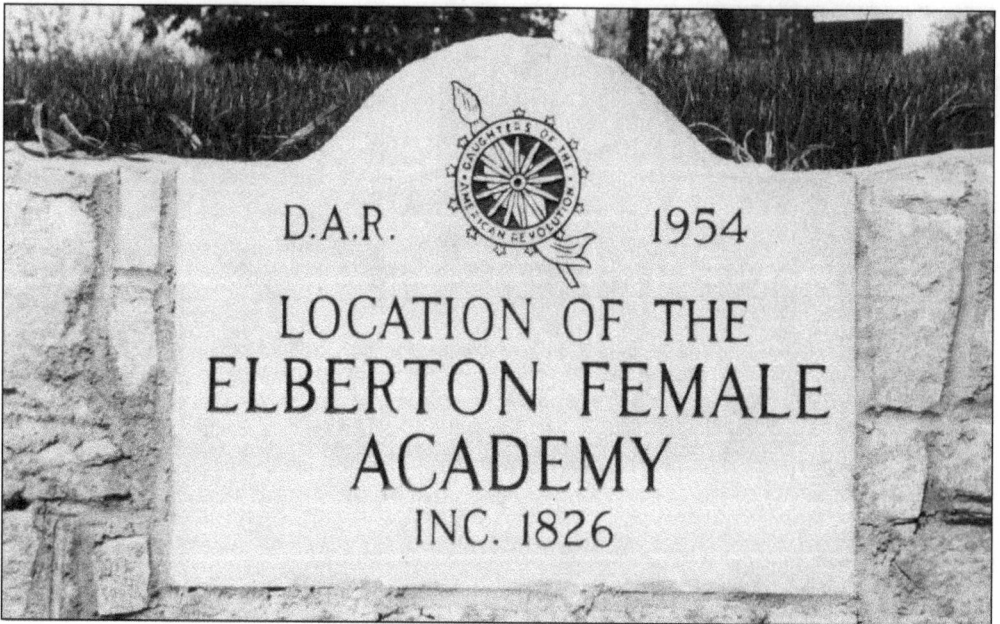

The Elberton Female Academy, one of many educational academies established in Elbert County by the Georgia Assembly, was located on South McIntosh Street but has long been demolished. The site is pinpointed by a 1954 DAR marker. One of the school's many illustrious students was writer Corra White Harris, born in Elbert County at Farmhill, near Middleton, where she spent much of her youth. (Courtesy of the *Elberton Star*.)

This house was rebuilt as a replica of the home of Joseph Rucker, using at least one major original log from the old structure, which was placed on the National Register of Historic Places in 1978. Rucker was president and organizer of the Bank of Ruckersville, which created its own currency. A prominent feature of the original house was the diamond pattern of brick in the chimney visible on the right side of the house in old photographs. The central, tree-lined alley leading up to its front door from the road is a striking element of this estate. (Photograph by the author.)

Four

CIVIL WAR ERA
AND AFTERMATH

In 1861, troops from Elbert County's regiments joined other Southern forces to fight in the Civil War. Many were wounded during the conflict, some fatally. Others returned to Elbert County after the war to resume their roles as sons, brothers, and fathers. Of those regiments that marched to war in 1861 or who joined later, many did not survive; but quite a few did, including the large contingent of Elbert County troops who were in the Virginia theater when the end came. As a consequence, Elbert County had many troops attached to companies serving with Gen. Robert E. Lee when he surrendered at Appomattox Courthouse in April 1865.

Although it had no Freedman's Bureau, Elbert County moved forward after the end of the Civil War. Cotton was a major crop grown throughout the county, on both small and large farms, with many tenant farmers growing cotton to sell and to use as payment for their housing during the year.

Dramatic changes occurred in transportation after the war ended. The county, which had been cut off from nearby areas for approximately a quarter century following the war, was opened to an expanded sphere when railroad service arrived in Elberton in 1878. The Elberton Air Line Railway, organized in 1871 at the primary instigation of Maj. J. H. Jones, was begun in 1873 and completed in 1878. Thomas J. Bowman, an acquaintance of Jones and a boarder at the Jones house, is credited with much of the effort to begin the train service. Dr. Dave Matthews, president of the company, was also a part of the team. Train service expanded from that point onward.

Education in the late 18th and early 19th centuries in the South consisted primarily of academies, but a number of tutors from the North taught children of wealthy Southerners. After the Civil War, however, numerous regional county schools began to appear. E. B. Tate, a Civil War veteran wounded severely by a minié ball, recovered and taught in one of the county schools in his early years before becoming a prosperous merchant and chairman of the Elbert County Commission, leading the effort for construction of the present Elbert County Courthouse.

By the end of the 19th century, prosperous merchants and professionals began to build grand houses on the road into Elberton. Today the road is named Heard Street and is part of the city. Also toward the end of the century, J. H. Orr established a photography studio on North McIntosh Street in Elberton, and for approximately two decades, he created an indelible set of images of both the sites and the faces of Elberton and Elbert County.

James Edward Herndon was extremely young when he served in the Civil War. His brother George Michael Herndon died in the Confederate army in 1862. (Courtesy of Lynda and Bob Farmer III.)

E. B. Tate, shown in old age wearing his Civil War medallion, was injured during the war but survived to teach in one of the many county schools set up during Reconstruction and later serve as the chairman of the Elbert County Board of Commissioners. It was during his term and under his guidance and direction that the Elbert County Courthouse was constructed. (Courtesy of Carolyn Miller.)

Joshua Freeman Auld built his Folk Victorian house on South McIntosh Street in Elberton around 1860 to 1870, after moving from South Carolina to work for the P. S. F. and Signey Bruce Carriage Shop in Ruckersville and remaining with the company when it moved to Elberton. In 1870, he bought the business and moved it to the corner of South McIntosh and Church Streets, just north of the house. He and his wife, the former Rachel McFall, had six children. (Photograph by the author.)

Bowman, a town in northwestern Elbert County that grew up after the construction of the road from Elberton to Toccoa in 1875, was chartered as a town on April 2, 1886, by the Superior Court of Elbert County. To accommodate train service, begun there in 1878, a depot was built and named for Col. Thomas J. Bowman, who surveyed the land around the railroad. Many of the late-19th- and early-20th-century buildings in Bowman still provide commercial space in this small, resort-like community. (Photograph by the author.)

Coldwater Methodist Church, begun by a number of socially prominent Methodists from Albemarle County, Virginia, was named by one of its famous occasional preachers, Bishop Francis Asbury, who stated that water from a spring on the Ralph Banks property produced true "cold water." The third sanctuary was a wooden frame building, erected in 1885 and replaced in 1947 by a solid brick structure. (Courtesy of Jean and Clyde Adams.)

The Free Classic Queen Anne style home of Lanita and Edward Phillips on Heard Street was built around 1890 by W. T. Arnold. (Photograph by the author.)

J. H. Orr's portrayal of judges and lawyers working in Elberton around 1880 to 1900 includes, from left to right, (first row) H. B. Payne; (second row) Judge Roebuck, Judge Meadow, Judge J. A. Worley, and Judge W. D. Tutt; (third row) Col. Z. B. Rogers, Sam Olive, Ira van Duzer, Tom Brown, and Judge George Grogan; (fourth row) C.P. Harris and Ted Sisk. (Courtesy of the Elbert County Historical Society.)

Elbert County veterans of the Civil War struggled over 30 years for a monument to their fallen comrades and commemorating their contributions. After monument fairs and other fund-raisers, they acquired a granite statue and base from Arthur Beter. (Courtesy of the *Elberton Star*.)

The widowed sisters-in-law of the Ann and Thomas Maxwell family posing for J. H. Orr are, from left to right, (first row) Emma Davis Maxwell, widow of John Matt Maxwell; Elizabeth Maxwell Mize Sorrells, widow of John Mize and Charles Sorrells; Drucilla Catherine Teasley Maxwell, widow of Martin Maxwell; (second row) Sally Maxwell Brown Rucker, widow of William B. Rucker and Roland J. Brown; Amelia Oglesby Maxwell, widow of William Hayden Maxwell; and Mary Caroline Fleming Maxwell, widow of Jackson Oliver Maxwell. (Courtesy of the Elbert County Historical Society.)

Artist Mary L. Eberhardt Oglesby (right), who painted watercolors, poses with her granddaughter Marie Chandler. (Courtesy of Lynda and Bob Farmer III.)

Mrs. Henry Epps of the Beverly community was only one of many Elbert County citizens who posed for James H. Orr. The artist inscribed the cards on which the photographs were mounted with his signature "J. H. Orr" label. (Courtesy of the author.)

41

The folk Victorian house of Rebecca Verner Auld and her husband, William Frederick Auld, is believed to date to about the time of their marriage in 1887. A second story was added to the original single-story building at some point. The home is now owned by descendant Frederick Auld, who lives in Fort Worth, Texas. (Photograph by the author.)

Robert and Mary Ann Palmer were cotton farmers in Flatwoods who also ground meal as part of their livelihood. Here they pose in front of part of their large acreage of cotton. (Courtesy of Lorene Godsey Brown and Jane Godsey Lunceford.)

Charles Fortson Herndon, shown in his youth in the 1890s, later opened Herndon's Drug Store in Elberton in 1910 and also served on the board of education in Elberton. (Courtesy of Lynda and Bob Farmer III.)

In 1894, the present building of Concord Church was erected on the site of the congregation's earlier structures—a brush arbor at first, a log cabin next, and then a second constructed building in 1845. This 1894 structure has had additions, including an annex built in 1924, installation of Rural Electrification Administration (REA) lights in 1936, and siding installed in 1937. In 1936, the congregation erected a granite marker honoring the donors of the church land. (Photograph by the author.)

Around 1896, Leila Oglesby Chandler, wife of James Chandler, sheriff of Elbert County from 1891 to 1895, posed with her children, from left to right, Carswell (Bubba), Marie, and Bertha, in Orr's studio. (Courtesy of Lynda and Bob Farmer III.)

The Wilhite Academy, in the heart of the Sweet City Community on modern-day Jones Ferry Road, was a simple wooden structure. Here in the 1890s, the student body poses in front of the building. (Courtesy of the *Elberton Star*.)

Five

PROGRESS AND PROBLEMS

In the early 20th century, Elbert County farmers grew cotton and took it to the primary market available to them, which, at the time, was located on the public square in Elberton. A group of cotton merchants would meet farmers in their crop-laden wagons to assess the quality of the cotton offered and determine prices they would pay for the cotton, which they would store in numerous warehouses built close to the railroad tracks. Some of the cotton was processed or, as it was called, compressed. From the warehouses, the cotton would be transported to other parts of the country and to other ports overseas. William Oscar Jones, one of the leading cotton merchants, kept an office in Liverpool, England, only one of the many destinations for this Elbert County crop. Many cotton growers were large planters; a few were small farmers. A significant number, though, lived as tenants on large estates of wealthy landowners and paid their yearly rent in cotton to the owners and settled other debts with the money they received for the small portion of the crop they were allowed to keep and sell.

In the 1920s, changes came to cotton farming almost overnight, with the appearance of the boll weevil, an insidious insect that destroyed the cotton plants and led to significantly deflated prices for the product at market. Many farmers continued to grow cotton, but a host of tenants found industrial work that paid wages for their labor in mills in Elberton or elsewhere in the county. One major mill in the Heardmont area was Pearle Mill, built close to the site of an earlier one. Its ownership changed several times, and, at some point, it was named Beverly Cotton Mill, with the small cluster of residences around it known as Beverly. To find wage-paying jobs, some farmers moved out of the county altogether, across the Savannah River, to work in mills in Calhoun Falls and Abbeville, South Carolina.

Sawmills, planing companies, and the brand-new and developing granite industry provided other employment. Granite sheds drew immigrant workers from Europe, particularly from Italy, because of the ongoing need for the skills of stonecutting, a well-known skill taught in Italy for centuries. Elberton also became a dominant mercantile center, drawing many shoppers traveling into town on the many incoming trains. The merchants enjoyed their wealth and displayed it in palatial residences in and on the way into the city.

Schools were located within the numerous communities of the county, although some were consolidated when possible; sports, especially baseball and basketball, were popular in and outside of these schools. Basketball was popular for both boys and girls, although, in the early years, only males had organized school-sponsored teams, while females had to establish their own teams and hire their own adult coaches.

In time, World War I, the Great Depression, and World War II intervened in the lives of Elbert County citizens, who withstood the conflicts and deprivations caused by these universal upheavals, as they had other earlier storms.

Ham Hall, who worked at both Pearle Mill in Heardmont (built by Elberton merchant Thomas M. Swift) and, in his later years, at the cotton mill in Elberton (also built by Swift) had been a noted baseball player at Heardmont in his youth. Here he rests in his buggy in front of the mill visible in the left background, whose ruins are now under water. (Courtesy of the author.)

George and Reba Gray lived in Heardmont, next to the post office. "Miss Reba," as Gray was known affectionately by her friends in the community, served as the postmistress of Heardmont for much of her adult life. This modern photograph shows changes and additions made by new residents of the Gray home. (Photograph by the author.)

Katherine McCall and Janesta McKinney write that Bethel Grove Baptist Church in Heardmont, originally part of Bethlehem Baptist (now Bethel E Baptist) Church, is the oldest African American church in Elbert County. (Photograph by the author.)

The W. R. (Bud) Ruff family home in the Falling Creek community was a Dutch Colonial–style timber house, adorned by a front dormer and a sloping front porch roof. A laid granite chimney dominates the western side of the house visible in the right foreground. (Photograph by the author.)

The Walton Smith Anderson family home at Double Bridges, in the Coldwater community, featured a constructional type of cross gables and was a typical farmhouse built around 1900. The surrounding fields were used for growing cotton, among other crops. (Courtesy of Iris and Gene Anderson.)

Built by Goshen John Bowers before 1906 and said to predate the town itself, the city now at the center of Bowman furnished water for the horses and mules of farmers bringing their crops into town to sell. (Courtesy of Lavonia Dickerson Turner.)

Will Shaw, Newt Crandon, and Sam Hall pose, from left to right, in front of the old Pearle Mill in the Beverly community, near Heardmont. (Courtesy of the author.)

White's Chapel Christian Methodist Episcopal Church was established in 1885. In 1905, on 5 acres purchased from Adeline Eberhardt Deadwyler, the congregation built this structure, which they named White's Chapel because three members of the original board were named White. Ben Sam White, Robert White, and Jackson White were some of the first trustees and lent their name to the congregation. (Photograph by the author.)

The community of Fortsonia was a thriving small village of stores for many years. The large store on the left was run by Guy Bell; the small one in the middle was Hudson's Store, run by Clark and Gilmer Hudson; and the store on the right was Fortson and Wyche, operated by Francis Benjamin Fortson and Mr. Wyche. (Photograph by the author.)

The house built on Heard Street for the William Snowden family later became the home of the Dr. Sid Johnson Sr. family for many years. Today it is the home of Iris and Gene Anderson, who have named it Isabella after her paternal grandmother. (Photograph by the author.)

The c. 1905–1906 Thornton house, located on the road to Elberton now named Heard Street, is neoclassical in style and is the home of Virginia and Carey Butler, who have owned and lived in it since 1979. (Photograph by the author.)

The 1906 L. W. Hendrick house, on Broad Street in Bowman, in later years was the longtime home of Martha Booth, who taught math and algebra throughout her teaching career in Elbert County. This neoclassical masterpiece is now the home of Holly Aguirre. (Photograph by the author.)

The lives of mill workers were strenuous, and hours were long. Here, mill hands, as the workers were called, pose in the spinning room at Pearle Mill, in the community called Beverly, during one its periods of operation. The ages of those working in the mill varied from young to old. (Courtesy of the author.)

The Daniel family lived at Ruckersville at the time this group photograph was taken in 1908. Gathered here at the home are, from left to right, (first row) three unidentified Daniel boys, Henry Willie Daniel, and a Daniel sister; (second row) Willie Henry Daniel, Anna Brooks Daniel, Beulah Daniel, unidentified, Bud Daniel, Leona Campbell Daniel holding an unidentified Daniel child, and Pammy N. Daniel. (Courtesy of Darlene West.)

In 1909, unidentified workers labored to erect a telephone pole on College Avenue in Elberton by using a system of pulleys. The C. J. Almand house, which was demolished later, can be seen in the center of the background. (Courtesy of the Elbert County Historical Society.)

Hardman School, often called "Hardaman School," constructed in 1909 as a replacement for the original school building of 1896, is shown in a modern fragmentary state. Located near Broad River, the school, constructed on the farm of Bud Hardman, provided educational facilities for students in this section of the western part of Elbert County. Hilda Moore (Fleming) attended here in the 1920s. (Courtesy of Martha Lee Jones.)

In 1910, the Seaboard Air Line built a brick passenger depot in Elberton that functions today as the home of the Elbert County Historical Society. When original plans called for a wooden building, civic and business leader William Oscar Jones traveled to the railroad corporate office in Norfolk, Virginia, and persuaded the company to build a brick depot, which was closed in 1971, after discontinuation of passenger train service to and from Elberton. (Courtesy of Bunnie and Stuart Lyle.)

Swift's Lithia Springs was a spa-like resort in the southeastern part of Elbert County owned by I. G. Swift. There, many from Heardmont and surrounding communities met for picnics and other social gatherings. The water from the spring was sold in bottles, which have become collectibles and can be found in some Elbert County collections. The site, which is still nearly intact, is the property of the Dan Dye family. (Photograph by the author.)

Logging work in the southeastern part of Elbert County was a strenuous job in the early 20th century. Sam Hall (second from right), who worked in many different jobs throughout the county, can be seen here while working at the sawmill with his unidentified fellow employees. (Courtesy of the author.)

The Elberton High School baseball team of 1911 poses in J. H. Orr's studio on the rug that appears in many of his photographs. In this photograph are, from left to right, (first row) Doc Harper and George Mattox; (second row) Bruce Harper, Jim Payne (manager), R. J. Ward (school principal), Burt Smith, and Starke Brewer; (third row) Joe Anderson, Brewer Tate, Herman Brown, James Wilcox, Virgil Sheppard, and Julian Brown. (Courtesy of the Elbert County Historical Society.)

Around 1913, students pose in front of the Heardmont School. (Courtesy of the author.)

Early-20th-century female sports teams in Elberton's Central School were not affiliated with the school. Instead the young women organized their own teams, selected their coaches, and identified themselves by the colors of their uniforms. Here the two groups are divided between the blue and gray group on the left and the black and red on the right. The colors were titles of their teams. The players are, from left to right, (first row) Mary Leslie Skelton, Olive Mattox, Mildred Payne, and Minnie Cohen; (second row) Steptoe Hubbard, Coach Florence Brown, Margaret Jones, and Bertha Gardner; (third row) Esther Carithers, Emeline Sheppard, Margaret Smith, and Mary Eakes; (fourth row) Louise Brown, Valeria Allen, Margaret Skelton, May Grogan, Gladys Allen, and Marion Wilcox. (Courtesy of the Elbert County Historical Society.)

The Dewy Rose School classes of 1911 pose in front of the school. The visible range in ages of students demonstrates the mix of students in small community schools throughout Elbert County. This building replaced a simpler one dating from 1896. According to John H. McIntosh, the Dewy Rose School began in 1852. (Courtesy of the Elbert County Historical Society.)

The Southern Railway completed two brick depots, freight and passenger, in Elberton in 1910; In 1986–1989, the Elbert County Historical Society restored the no-longer-used passenger depot for their permanent headquarters. In 1990, the society acquired a metal caboose and tracks from the Norfolk Southern Railroad and set it up on the western side of the depot, for use as a tourist attraction. It was open for tours at the May 2010 centennial celebration of the depot. (Photograph by the author.)

In 1917, Blackwell Bridge, named after the man who gave access to the bridge from his land, was constructed over Beaverdam Creek in Heardmont. In January 1984, the old bridge was moved by the U.S. Army Corps of Engineers to a new protected site, near Coldwater Creek, to save it from the waters impounded by the soon to be completed Richard B. Russell Dam. (Courtesy of the Elbert County Historical Society.)

The girls' basketball team of 1918 poses in front of the Elberton High School and now is part of the Elberton High School program, as suggested by their official-looking uniforms and their basketball inscribed "EHS-18." The players here include, from left to right, (first row) Frances Mattox, Rachel Strickland, and Mozelle Jones; (second row) J. Chandler Turner, Emmie Lee Whiteside, Willie Rich, Janie Auld, Mary Thomas Maxwell, and Rebecca Berman. (Courtesy of the Elbert County Historical Society.)

In 1921, H. L. Wiggs, a leading member of the rapidly developing granite industry in Elberton, built a Tudor house on Forest Avenue; until 1931, his family occupied the residence, which later became the home of the late Helen Turner. (Photograph by the author.)

The Bowman United Methodist Church is a brick building constructed in 1925 to replace a frame building from the late 19th century located on this site. The frame structure was built on this lot donated by William Burden to provide better facilities for the congregation, which had met in a log building for a few years following the establishment of the church in 1875. (Photograph by the author.)

The Reverend Emile Robert Goss was a circuit rider in Elbert County who, during his 40 years of service, traveled to many local churches in the county and even to some in South Carolina. His grave marker in the Bowman City Cemetery lists the names of the many churches he served in Elbert County and elsewhere, including the two South Carolina churches listed at the bottom of his marker. (Courtesy of Pat Jarvis.)

Truck driver Fred Matthew Hall Jr. stands on the Georgia-South Carolina Memorial Bridge on the day it opened on Armistice Day 1927. After the completion of the bridge, which connected the two states, Hall, like others, was able to drive over the Savannah River, instead of taking one of many risk-filled ferries crossing its often treacherous waters. The Memorial Bridge was replaced by a modern version during construction of the Richard B. Russell Dam project. (Courtesy of Tracie York.)

The 1929 Rock Branch Baptist Church is the third structure built for this congregation, which was founded in 1845 and included the Reverend Asa Chandler as one of its members. (Photograph by the author.)

In 1929, the Bowman school district voted bonds to construct a school building for elementary and high school grades. The building survived until it burned in 1969. (Courtesy of Lavonia Dickerson Turner.)

The *Elberton Star* noted that some 400 businessmen and guests gathered in the old Central School/ Elberton High School (burned in 1955) for the Elberton Chamber of Commerce banquet on January 23, 1931. At the head table are, from left to right, T. O. Tabor Jr., Raymond Stapleton, Fred Herndon, L. R. Power, Furman Smith, Charlie Compton, H. P. Hunter, Tom Gaines, and Boozer Payne. The chamber was organized in 1909 and survived into the mid-teens, although it struggled for existence. Finally in the early 1920s, it was reorganized and continues today as the Elbert County Chamber of Commerce. (Courtesy of the Elbert County Chamber of Commerce.)

In 1932, the Bowman Baptist Church built this brick structure to replace its original frame church. The congregation, established in 1789, grew by leaps and bounds and made additions to its original structure and began planning this new building in 1924. (Photograph by the author.)

In 1936, Iris Anderson's parents bought the Haslett house, dated c. 1800, facing the original Athens Highway. Mrs. Haslett, though, rejected an offer to reorient it when a new highway was built behind it. Facing the new highway, large white stone letters spelled out "TATE'S PLACE," a combined café, dance hall, and tourist court owned by Anderson's grandfather on the opposite side of the highway. (Courtesy of Iris and Gene Anderson.)

Corra White Harris, noted author, whose first book, titled *The Circuit Rider's Wife*, was based somewhat on her experiences and later made into a film, was born at Farm Hill, a 2,000-acre cotton farm near Middleton whose plantation house burned before her father inherited the property. She and her family thus lived in the old overseer's house. This granite marker erected by the Sorosis Club in 1926 identifies the entrance to the farm site. (Photograph by the author.)

63

The Daniel women dominate this family grouping at their home in Fortsonia. In this image are, from left to right, (first row) Sibyl, Mattie, Herman, and their dog Danny; (second row) Mrs. James William Daniel and Edna. (Courtesy of Darlene West.)

Pete Wells grew up in Heardmont and later moved to Calhoun Falls, South Carolina, when his family left tenant farming to work in the mill after the boll weevil affected their ability to earn a living growing cotton. He stands on the Georgia-South Carolina Memorial Bridge connecting Elbert County to Calhoun Falls. (Courtesy of the author.)

Ocie Christian Eaves and her family lived on Ruckersville Road, as one of the early residential families of the community that became Sunny Acres. This community has now developed extensively with the addition of more residents, Beaverdam Elementary School, and the Francis Asbury Methodist Church. (Courtesy of the author.)

In 1933, the Sinclair Oil Company built a service station on the eastern side of the public square, on the site of the old store owned by William Oscar Jones, who died in 1931. After serving as the site of other later businesses, the building is now home to the Elbert County Chamber of Commerce. (Courtesy Elbert County Chamber of Commerce.)

Floyd Godsey, a major cotton farmer in Flatwoods, poses with his hunting dogs in front of the smokehouse, where he cured hams after killing hogs on the first cold days of the fall and winter season. (Courtesy of Lorene Godsey Brown and Jane Godsey Lunceford.)

Six

POSTWAR PROSPERITY

After World War II ended, quite a few service personnel returned to build homes or, in many cases, live in apartments with their new spouses, building families. Postwar prosperity soon led to rapid development of residential construction to accommodate the expanding population growth of the baby boom. As wartime restrictions on both new construction and resources eased, and residential areas as well as the business and entertainment sectors thrived, Elberton and Elbert County began to witness the optimism and prosperity for which the postwar years are noted. In 1947, the Elberton radio station added entertainment and information facilities to the community, and the Elberton Country Club expanded the field of entertainment for the private sector. A small airport added another transportation choice for some, and master photographer Everett Saggus came to Elberton and created a detailed chronicle of the lives of Elbertonians for the next 30 years.

Commercial growth in Elberton after the war was steady but lacked much of the intense fervor of the early 20th century, although the granite industry began its greatest expansion during the postwar era. In the early 1950s, B. Frank Coggins Sr. began to investigate the feasibility of strengthening the granite industry for financial benefit. He led the incorporation movement of the Elberton Granite Association, Inc., which quickly enabled the sector to grow into the mammoth industry it became by the end of the 20th century.

Educational development continued apace, with the expansion of the Elberton school system into a county-wide system in 1958 and racial integration that began in the 1960s and was complete by 1970. School sports and the accompanying rituals of homecoming events and citizen participation in their promotion led to the construction of the Granite Bowl. It is a football field special to Elberton because of its native granite installed in tiers around its playing field by local granite workers. The location of the Granite Bowl is historical, too, because the cool springs that drew mid-18th-century settlers to Elberton were located in the old grown-over ravine, which the city cleared to make way for the Granite Bowl. Begun in 1954 by Ben Sutton, head of Elberton City Parks, the park that evolved into the Granite Bowl received major additions in 1961 and some minor ones in later years. The site is now a premier attraction for visitors as well as residents of the city and county.

Service organizations and cultural groups thrived during this period, and historical preservation began to attract followers. The Elbert County Historical Society was formed in 1975–1976 and later earned nominations on the National Register of Historic Places for buildings in the city and county. Meanwhile, Elberton acquired a Main Street program and continued to focus on its historic sites. These efforts served to engage the community in its collective heritage and continue its interest in preservation for future generations.

One of the early postwar buildings was the Elberton Country Club, designed by J. Hunter Price, whose architectural rendering appeared in the *Elberton Star* shortly after the foundation had been laid in June 1947. It shows the club on its pine-covered knoll, set on 122 acres on Country Club Road, just off the Lexington Highway. (Courtesy of the *Elberton Star*.)

In the late 1940s, Grady Thrasher of the Thrasher Brothers Aerial Circus performed aerial feats at the old Elberton Airport on Calhoun Falls Highway. The Armory Auditorium is presently located where the airport used to be. (Courtesy of Randy Haralson.)

Jack D. Moore, who was in charge of the Carlton Bridge Weather Station near the Broad River, was known as the first weatherman in Elbert County. On his residential property, located close to the Broad River in the western part of the county, he kept the specially fitted box shown here, from which he obtained pertinent data and mailed information concerning weather changes to the federal government. (Courtesy of Martha Lee Jones.)

In 1947, Elberton High School received a new training car for its driver education program. Here superintendent Marvin Hardy Jr. accepts the keys to the new car from J. W. McLanahan of McLanahan Chevrolet Company. Gathered for the event in front of the Elberton High School are, from left to right, Ruth McMullan, Pilot Club; Dr. Charles Johnson, Rotary Club; Herbert Moore, Kiwanis Club; James Cleveland, Exchange Club; J. W. McLanahan; Marvin Hardy Jr.; Zack McLanahan of McLanahan Chevrolet Company; and Grayson Hill, school principal. (Courtesy of Shirley and Walter McNeely.)

Taking part in the new spirit of fun and relaxation after the tense war years, many families held reunions and other social outings. Here the Haynie family youth posed at one of their picnic reunions are, from left to right, (first row) unidentified, Waymon Miller, unidentified, Kathleen Hall, unidentified, and Nancy Haynie; (second row) Bobbie Sue Martin, Jane Godsey, Elizabeth Higginbotham, Rosemary Haynie, Lorene Godsey, and unidentified. (Courtesy of Lorene Godsey Brown and Jane Godsey Lunceford.)

In 1950, Juanita Dickerson (left), Miriam Dickerson (center), and Ed Dickerson (partly hidden at right) pose on the new bridge over Beaverdam Creek in Bowman. The creek, not far from where the Dickerson family lived, was a site for recreational bathing, as well as baptismal dips for a time. (Courtesy of Lavonia Dickerson Turner.)

The Elbert Memorial Hospital was opened in 1950 as the Elberton-Elbert County Hospital in a building constructed partly with funds from the Hill-Burton Act. Patient rooms were either private, with one bed, or semiprivate, with two beds. This room on the third floor is typical of the private rooms with simple furnishings that filled the hospital in its early years. The hospital was renamed in 1985 to honor the services of its doctors, nurses, and staff and the many gifts the hospital had received. (Courtesy of the Elbert Memorial Hospital Foundation.)

Woodrow Jones (right) owned and operated Jones Maytag Company on Heard Street, across from the old First Baptist Church, and then moved to a second location, closer to the square. In this early 1950s image, from left to right, Russell Butler, the first Elberton High School Diversified Cooperative Training (DCT) student in 1946; George Ward; and Donnie Whitner, a DCT student at the time, take apart an automatic washing machine timer for one of Jones's clients. (Courtesy of the *Elberton Star*.)

George T. Oglesby was the first president of the Elberton Granite Association, Inc., serving in the 1951–1952 period and returning to the position later in the decade, in 1955–1956. (Courtesy of Tom Oglesby.)

In 1952, Carolyn Miller (center) was selected to represent Georgia in the Cherry Blossom Festival in Washington, D.C., and ride in the festival parade in a float sponsored by the Elberton Granite Association, Inc. Here her mother, Corra Jane Tate Miller (kneeling, right), and her aunt Carrie Sophia Tate (left) make final touches on one of the two gowns she wore during the festival. (Photograph by master photographer Everett Saggus; courtesy of Carolyn Miller.)

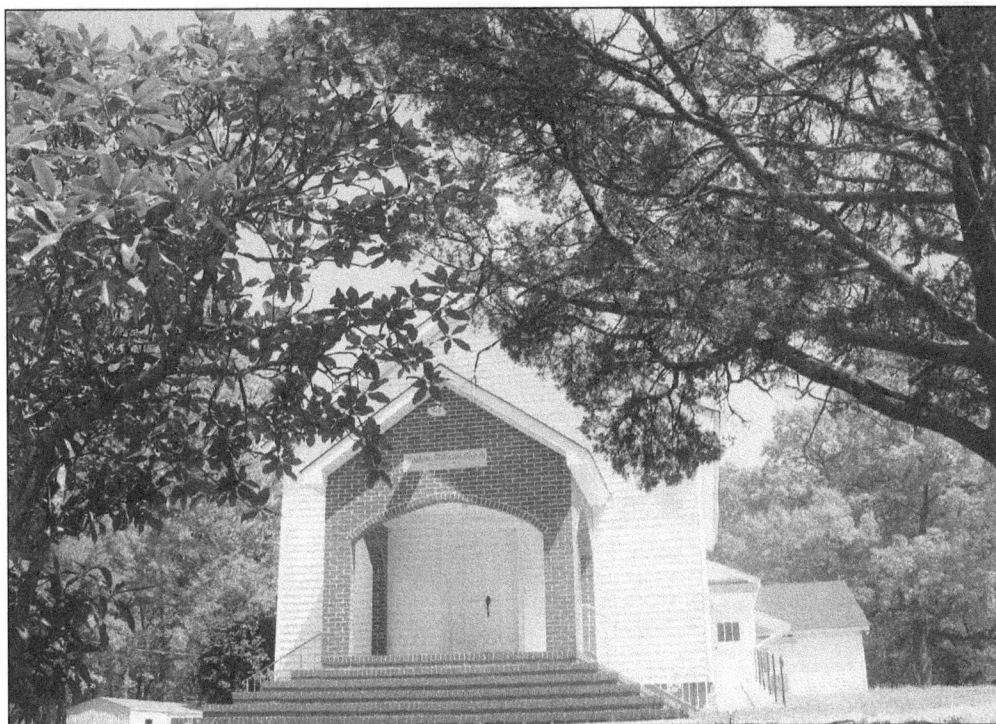

Middleton United Methodist Church was established in 1873; for many years, its first structure was called "Eureka." The present modern structure is set on a high hill, with a commanding view of the surrounding picturesque countryside. In the late 19th century, the church was used as a school for a few years; one of its students was the future writer Corra White Harris. (Photograph by the author.)

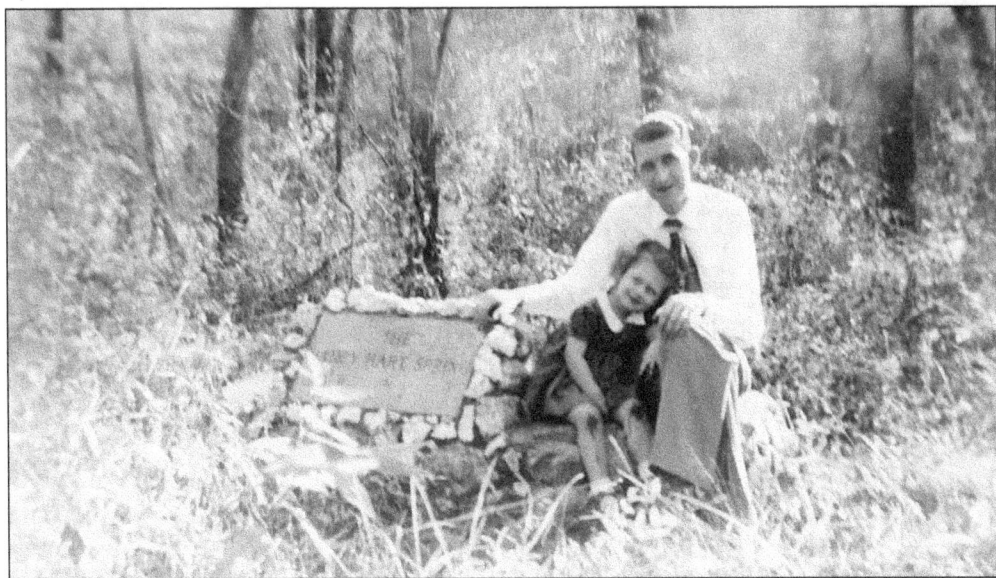

Marvin Rathbone (right) sits quietly with his daughter Deborah at the Nancy Hart Spring near the patriot's cabin, while visiting shortly after the cabin was opened for tourists in the early 1950s. (Courtesy of Pat and Marvin Rathbone.)

The Elberton High School football team of 1953–1954 appears in front of the clubhouse at the old practice field. Players are, from left to right, (first row) Johnny Goss, Joel Seymour, Gene Jordan, Cecil Smith, Ronald Martin, Gerald Glass, and Curtis Allgood; (second row) Larry Wilson, John

Galli, Donald Norman, Rod Daniel, Starke Lovinggood, Jimmy Edwards, James Noggle, and Ronald Norman; (third row) Bob Lamb, Bob Farmer Jr., Ronald Nativi, Walter Eaves, Jerry Ray, Joe Fields, and Gene Edwards. (Courtesy of Lynda and Bob Farmer III.)

At Georgia Teachers College (now Georgia Southern University), Chester Webb was a 1955–1956 Helms All-American basketball player and member of the *Atlanta Journal-Constitution* Collegiate All-State basketball team (1952–1956). He remains the all-time leading scorer and rebounder in the school's men's basketball history. His no. 22 was retired in January 2010. (Courtesy of Carol and Chester Webb.)

For the 1954–1955 season, the heart of the Elberton High School basketball team, the so-called "A" string, consisted of the starting five shown below in the Armory Auditorium. They are, from left to right, Bobby Smith, Eddie Roberts, James Bettis, Bob Farmer Jr., and Larry Wilson. (Courtesy of Lynda and Bob Farmer III.)

Carolyn Miller (first row, center) became the girls' basketball coach at Elberton High School in 1954 and led her teams to two straight years without a loss, with a total of 36 consecutive victories. In this photograph of the 1954–1955 Elberton High School girls' basketball team and coach are, from left to right, (first row) Furmadeen Angel, Freida Allgood, Charlene Bass, Coach Miller, Patsy Neal (later a star college player and member of the U.S. medal-winning squad in the 1959 Pan American Games and now a member and executive director of the Women's Basketball Hall of Fame in Knoxville, Tennessee), Angela Ambrosini, and Bettie Bundrick; (second row) Shirley Norman, Geraldine Brown, Martha Ann Brady, Ann Johnson, Judy Ray, Ann Williams, Mary Alice Smith, Vivian Bundrick, Anne Dow, and manager Peggy McDonald. (Courtesy of Carolyn Miller.)

The Bowman High School girls' team and coach poses in 1954–1955 for an official photograph. They are, from left to right, (first row) Jane Ashworth, Joyce Lunsford, Doris Kidd, Laverne Massey, Geraldine Brady, and Patty Seymour; (second row) Nancy Mize, Mary Jane Wood, Marie Carey, Nedra Thurmond, Naomi Brown, and Jane Skelton; (third row) Sylvia Maxwell, Diane David, coach Earl Perry, Lavonia Dickerson, and Rachel Beasley. (Courtesy of Lavonia Dickerson Turner.)

Eighth graders Jane Davis and Jenny Carol Rice take a break during recess at Doves Creek School (formerly Wilhite Academy) in March 1957, the next to last year the school was open for classes. (Courtesy of the author.)

In the afternoon, the Elberton High School homecoming court assembled in the parking lot of the First United Methodist Church to prepare for the homecoming parade of the fall 1956 season. Wearing their evening gowns, the court consisted of, from left to right, Sondra Martin, Suzanne Auld, Ann Williams, Lanie Lunsford, Marion Ann Herndon, Margaret Ann Stephens, Gail Daniel, Carolyn Childs, and Jackie Bradford. (Courtesy of Lynda and Bob Farmer III.)

At night, Elberton fans cheered the Elberton Blue Devils in the homecoming game. Seated in the first row are members of the homecoming court. They are, from left to right, homecoming queen Ann Williams, Lanie Lunsford ("Miss Blue Devil"), Jackie Bradford, Sondra Martin, Suzanne Auld, Margaret Ann Stephens, Carolyn Childs, Marion Ann Herndon, and Gail Daniel. (Courtesy of Lynda and Bob Farmer III.)

Captains Bobby H. Smith (left), Bob Farmer Jr. (center), and Cecil Smith huddle and lead the Elberton High School Blue Devils during the 1956 season. (Courtesy of Lynda and Bob Farmer III.)

Adger Moore (left), who served as sheriff of Elbert County from 1957 to 1976, poses with deputy sheriff Alton McCarty (right) just outside the old sheriff's office and Elbert County Jail. (Photograph by master photographer Everett Saggus; courtesy of Shirley and Walter McNeely.)

Bob Farmer Jr., who was described by fellow athlete Powell Gaines as an almost perfect player during his years playing sports for the Elbert County Blue Devils, was the first player at Elberton High School to letter in five sports. He earned the honor during one academic year, 1956–1957. (Courtesy of Lynda and Bob Farmer III.)

In 1957, the Elberton Granite Association, Inc., purchased a station wagon in what their magazine, *The Elberton Graniteer*, dubbed as "appropriate 'granite gray.' " Here George Gaines (right), president of the association, hands the keys over to William A. Kelly, general manager (later executive vice president) of the association at the time. (Courtesy of the Elberton Granite Association, Inc.)

Granite workers attend the annual membership meeting of the Elberton Granite Association, Inc., held June 10, 1958, at the Elberton Country Club. General manager William A. Kelly (far right) is on hand to verify that all activities, including the charbroiling of the steaks, are going well. (Courtesy of the *Elberton Star*.)

The Bowman Senior Choral Group performed on WJBF-TV in Augusta as part of an Elbert County 4-H event during the 1957–1958 school year at Bowman School. Members of the group are, from left to right, (first row) Nancy Brown, Nancy Mize, and Glenda Fleming; (second row) Lavonia Dickerson, Beth Rice, Hortense Maxwell, Carol Scott, Delina Seigler, Juanita Smith, Dianne David, and Sylvia Maxwell. (Courtesy of Lavonia Dickerson Turner.)

In 1958–1959, Hattie Mae Edwards's eighth-grade class at Falling Creek School created a newspaper titled the *Boomerang*. Here editors scan media for items to include in categories listed on the wall. Members of the staff are, from left to right, (first row) Beth Edwards, Connie Baggett, and Elaine Rhodes; (second row) Susan Todd, Mary Jane Kimbrough, Joyce M. Davis, teacher Hattie Mae Edwards, and Carolyn Brown. (Courtesy of the *Elberton Star*.)

In February 1959, the Elberton Granite Association, Inc., held a four-day conference, co-sponsored by the University of Georgia, at the Georgia Center for Continuing Education in Athens and at various granite sites in Elberton. Here conferees tour one of many Elberton finishing plants. George T. Oglesby (fifth from left) accompanies the tour group. (Photograph by master photographer Everett Saggus, courtesy of the *Elberton Star.*)

In August 1960, the month designated Tourist Promotion Month by the Elberton Chamber of Commerce, W. F. Grant (left) invited Pat Gidden (second from left) and Sonny Gidden (third from left) of Forest Park Memorials in Houston, Texas, to the Elberton Granite Association when they were on their way home from a granite convention in Cincinnati. Here the Giddens are being shown a sample of "Berkeley Blue" granite by John Coggins, vice president of Coggins Granite Industries. (Courtesy of the *Elberton Star.*)

Paul Brown served the 10th Congressional District of Georgia in the U.S. House of Representatives from 1933 to 1961. He retired early in 1961 and died later that year. At the time of his retirement, he was awarded the granite plaque shown here for his illustrious career and public service to Elbert County and his entire district. The portrait on the plaque was carved by granite sculptor Richard Cecchini. (Courtesy of the Elberton Granite Association, Inc.)

Danny Turner poses in September 1962 on the sorrel he entered in the Fourth Annual Elberton Horse Show, which was sponsored by the Elberton Pilot Club. (Courtesy of the *Elberton Star*.)

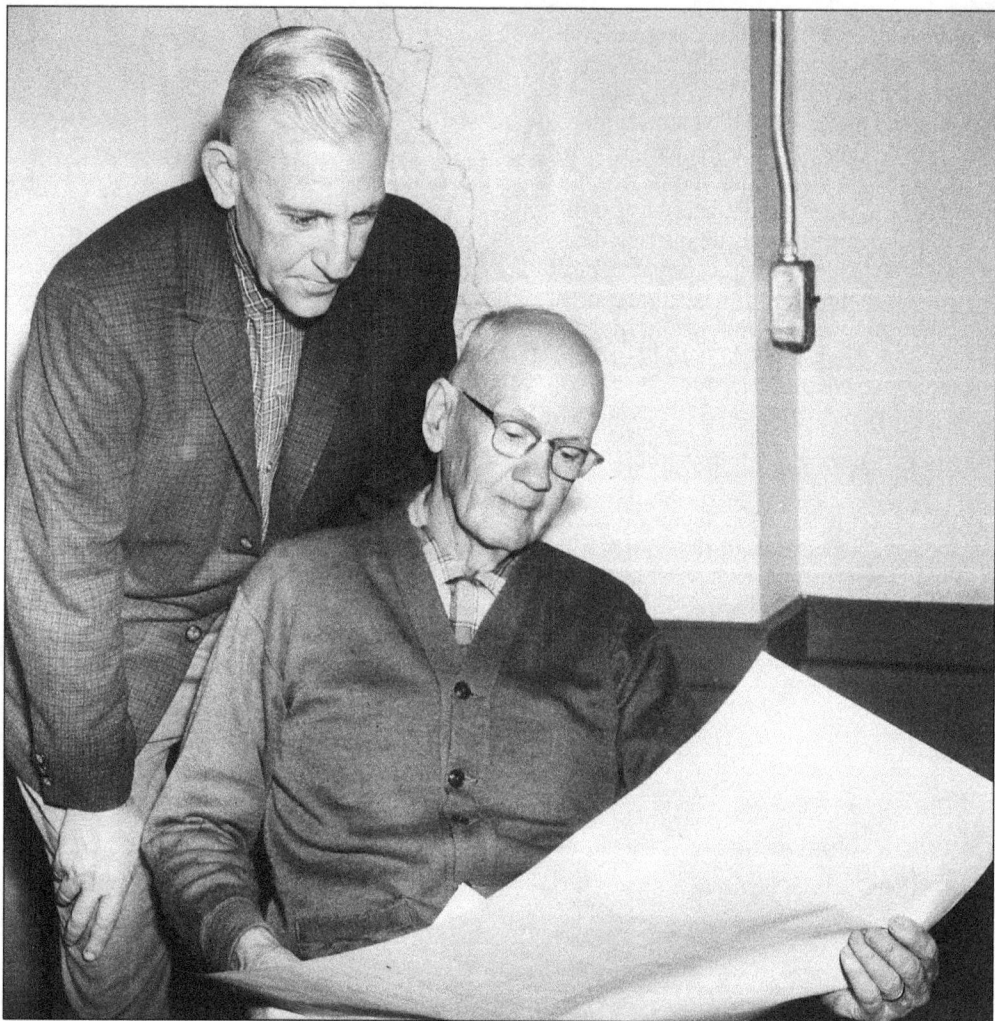

In 1962, Elbert County created a new and enlarged ballot for November voting. Here Tom Rucker (left), clerk of the Elbert County Superior Court, and Thomas Hewell Sr., chairman of the Elbert County Democratic Executive Committee, discuss how long voters will need to stand to complete the long ballot. Rucker served a total of 37 years as clerk and deputy clerk, having begun in 1931 as deputy to his father, Billy Rucker, who served from 1901 to 1945. Tom Rucker was elected to office after his father's death and never missed a term of court before retiring in 1968. (Courtesy of the *Elberton Star.*)

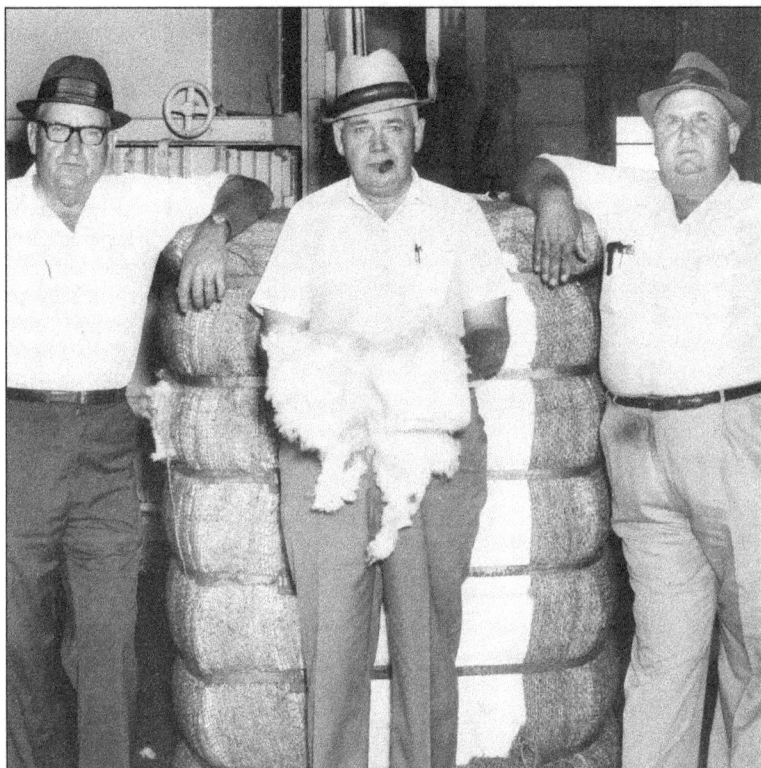

In August 1968, Floyd Godsey (right) presented the first bale of cotton for ginning in Elbert County for the year of 1968. The cotton was ginned by Temple and Ayers on the old Middleton Road. Glenn Ayers (left) and J. D. Temple (center) inspect the cotton to determine its grade and weight. (Courtesy of Lorene Godsey Brown and Jane Godsey Lunceford.)

On November 5, 1968, voting was heavy and lines were long throughout the day as Elbert County voters came to the courthouse to choose among Richard Nixon, Hubert Humphrey, and George Wallace for president of the United States, one of many races decided by voters that day. (Courtesy of the *Elberton Star*.)

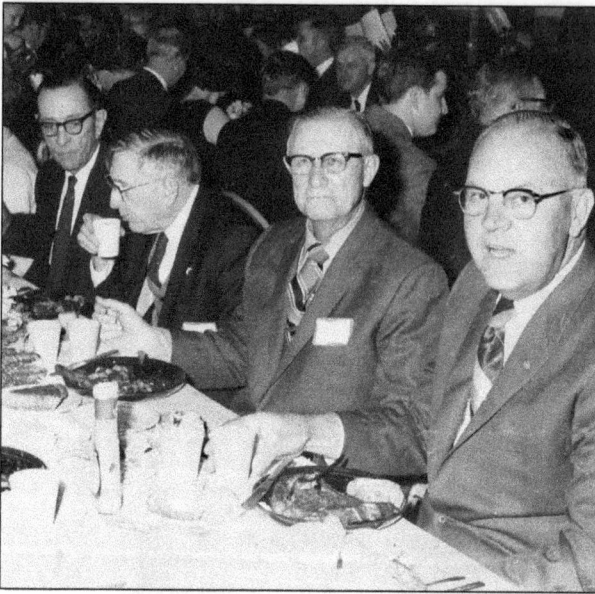

At the chamber of commerce banquet in March 1970, more than 500 guests met, and some reestablished old friendships. Among those at the event were, from left to right, Henry Hill, retired Seaboard Coast Line employee; W. Angus Lee, another retiree; Yates Ross, former railroad agent in Elberton; and James Cleveland, vice president of the Granite City Bank, participating in the festivities of the 46th annual banquet. (Courtesy of the *Elberton Star.*)

In 1971, Harry Miller (right), Elberton Coca-Cola Company owner, was honored with the Per Capita Sales Award for the district containing Elberton. L. B. Etheredge (left), district manager of Coca-Cola USA, made the presentation to Miller for his high sales of the company's product in the Elberton territory for the previous year. (Courtesy of the *Elberton Star.*)

Freeman Leverett served the city and county as one of its premier attorneys and was noted, too, for his cultural interests. He served as foreign student committee chairman in the Elberton Rotary Club and made two trips, with his wife, to Russia. He shared experiences of his travels with the public by presenting a program for the Elbert County Historical Society on his journeys. Leverett was known as well for his service to others. On at least two occasions, he used his ham radio operator expertise to provide contact for local Americans with some of their family members without access to ordinary means of communication while abroad. (Courtesy of the *Elberton Star*.)

The Westside Community Aid Club No. 2 was formed for prayer and community aid in the late 1950s by Colonial Thornton. Initially membership had been limited to women only, and men were added later. In this photograph are, from left to right, (first row) Charity M. Geter, Lady B. McLendon, Susie Willis, Fannie Bell, Joe Harper, Emily Callaway, Katherine Hall, Cassie Smith, Doris Smith, and Ruby Hunt; (second row) Beatrice Sims, Effie Willingham, Willie Syphore, Belinda Burton, Norman Downer, Roy Hall, Elizabeth Heard, and Willie Heard. (Courtesy of Rhonda Callaway.)

In 1970, Dr. D. N. Thompson (right), a family doctor who practiced medicine for more than 60 years, treated 58-year-old Jesse W. Almond. Almond was a marble mason at Arlington National Cemetery whom Dr. Thompson had delivered in the early days of his practice. (Courtesy of the *Elberton Star*.)

In the early 1980s, the Veterans of Foreign Wars installed the following officers: (first row) Bill Shields, Gene Bell, Eddie Todd, and Clinton Brown; (second row) Dallas Webb, Shorty North, Monjet Higginbotham, and Ralph Cordell. (Courtesy of the *Elberton Star*.)

In 1981, the ladies of Elberton Office Supply posed for the promotion of National Secretaries Week. Seated is Margaret Mann; standing are, from left to right, Betty Ann Craft, Teresa Haston, and Virginia Butler. (Courtesy of the *Elberton Star*.)

In 1981, Clyde Adams (left) presented the award for Farmer of the Year to the father-and-son team of Jack Grant (center) and his son Bruce. The honor was bestowed at the Annual Farm-City Banquet, and the honorees were cited at the Elbert County Chamber of Commerce banquet the following spring. (Courtesy of the *Elberton Star*.)

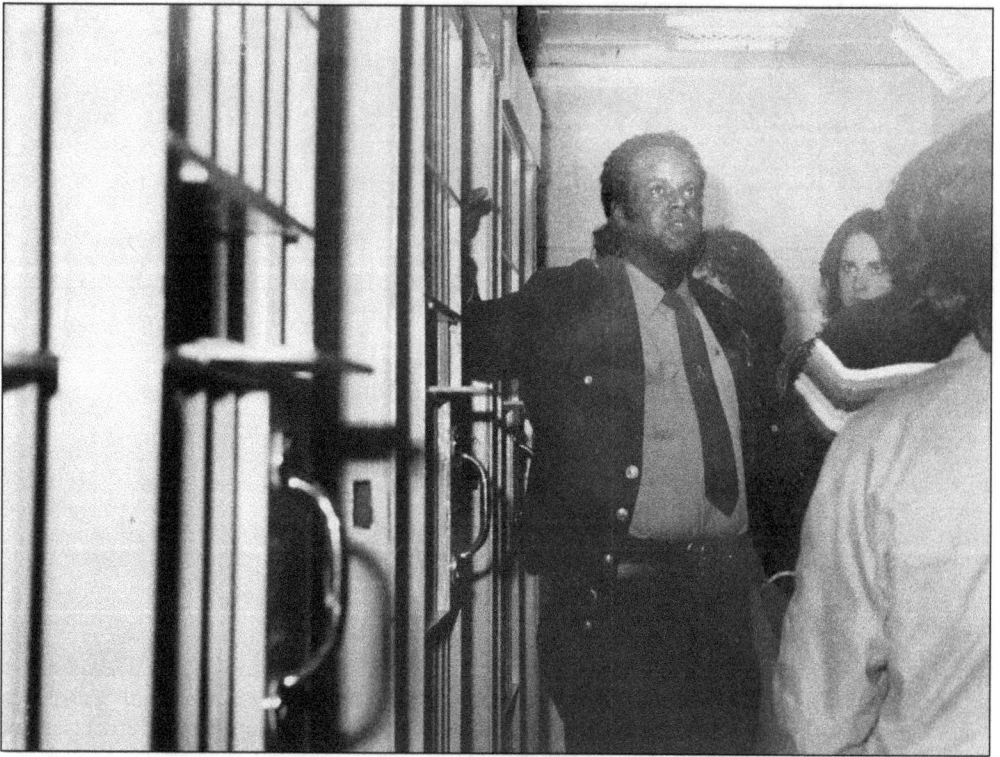

In 1979, police officer John Hubbard, now retired and serving as an Elbert County commissioner, presented a tour of the Elberton City Jail to a class from Elbert County Comprehensive High School. (Courtesy of the *Elberton Star*.)

Otis Vickery (second from left) receives his honorary service award from an unidentified district manager (second from right), as his coworkers Ralph Jordan (left), Jimmy Johnson (right), and Charles Johnson (back row) look on. (Courtesy of the *Elberton Star*.)

Gene Anderson (center)—game warden for 25 years beginning in 1960, sergeant from 1971 onward, and sheriff of Elbert County from 1997 to 2000—is honored by the Georgia Department of Natural Resources for his service to the state. Department of Natural Resources commissioner J. Leonard Ledbetter (left) and game and fish director Leon Kirkland (right) make the presentation. (Courtesy of the *Elberton Star*.)

In April 1970, the Elbert County Wildlife Association sponsored the Clark Hill White Bass Tournament. The winners shown here included, from left to right, (first row) Donald Dean, second prize; Max Beard, second prize; Charles Cecchini, first prize; and Leroy Jones, fourth prize; (second row) Bobby Jones, fourth prize; Lawrence Cecchini, first prize; Jim Thomas, third and first prizes with the largest hybrid; and David Williams, third prize. (Courtesy of the *Elberton Star*.)

Herbert Wilcox was a noted chronicler of Elbert County history. As a writer for the *Elberton Star*, he recounted stories of historical significance, folklore, and pure wit. His articles later formed the basis of *Georgia Scribe*, published in 1974. (Photograph by master photographer Everett Saggus; courtesy of the Elbert County Historical Society.)

Irene Stilwell Wilcox (married to Herbert Wilcox), daughter of the teacher for whom Stilwell School in Elberton was named, wrote a long series of articles about historical sites and individuals throughout Elbert County in the late 1970s and early 1980s. Her accounts of life of Elberton and Elbert County in the past reminded mature Elbertonians of events in the county's past and provided a window to that time for those too young to remember it. (Courtesy of the *Elberton Star*.)

The Knee-Hi Baseball champions of Elbert County in 1979 were the Eagles. The winning players, their coach, and team mother are, from left to right, as follows: (first row) Kevin Swicegood, Bryan Acker, Justin Fleming, and Dave Johnson; (second row) Jay Hunt, John McMullan, Denny Seymour; (third row) coach Jerry Smith and Vonda Moon, team mother. (Courtesy of the *Elberton Star*.)

Carol Fernandez (left) and Linda Rice (right) guard the ball carrier from the opposing team in a rousing game played in the Inferno, the basketball gymnasium built in 1968. (Courtesy of the *Elberton Star.*)

Barry Calhoun practices for the rough and tumble of the football games of the Elbert County Comprehensive High School Blue Devils. (Courtesy of the *Elberton Star*.)

In 1980, DAR members, from left to right, Clara Mae Algood, Carolyn Miller, and Jane Scarborough dedicated a granite marker in honor of Flatwoods Academy, established 1868 in the Fortsonia community on part of an old Revolutionary battlefield. Students drawn from families who settled the Flatwoods area included ancestors of many Elbert County citizens as well as Carrie Mae Hudson Tate, great-grandmother of these DAR members. The school burned in 1925. (Courtesy of Carolyn Miller.)

In 1981, at the old Hanks Cattleman Restaurant on Elbert Street, heart fund chairman Billy Ray Brown (right) was presented a medallion in appreciation of his work with the heart fund, while then-assistant city attorney Steve Jenkins (left) congratulated him on his good works. (Courtesy of the *Elberton Star*.)

In 1982, the Elberton Granite Association, Inc., dug up Dutchy, the Elbert County Civil War veterans' granite statue that, in 1900, was dismantled, broken below the knees, and buried on the town square. Here from left to right, Mayor Joe Fendley, EGA executive vice president William A. Kelly, Wayne Mullenix (who helped excavate the statue), and an unidentified photographer examine statue fragments being cleaned for display in the Elberton Granite Museum and Exhibit. (Courtesy of the *Elberton Star.*)

On National Register Recognition Day in November 1982, the Elbert County Historical Society announced new nominations for historic districts in the city, including some business structures in the city and some residential districts. On hand for the event were, from left to right, (first row) Mary Jean Eaves, society president; Merle Wyche, chair of Recognition Day, and Ed Mims. (Courtesy of Elbert County Historical Society.)

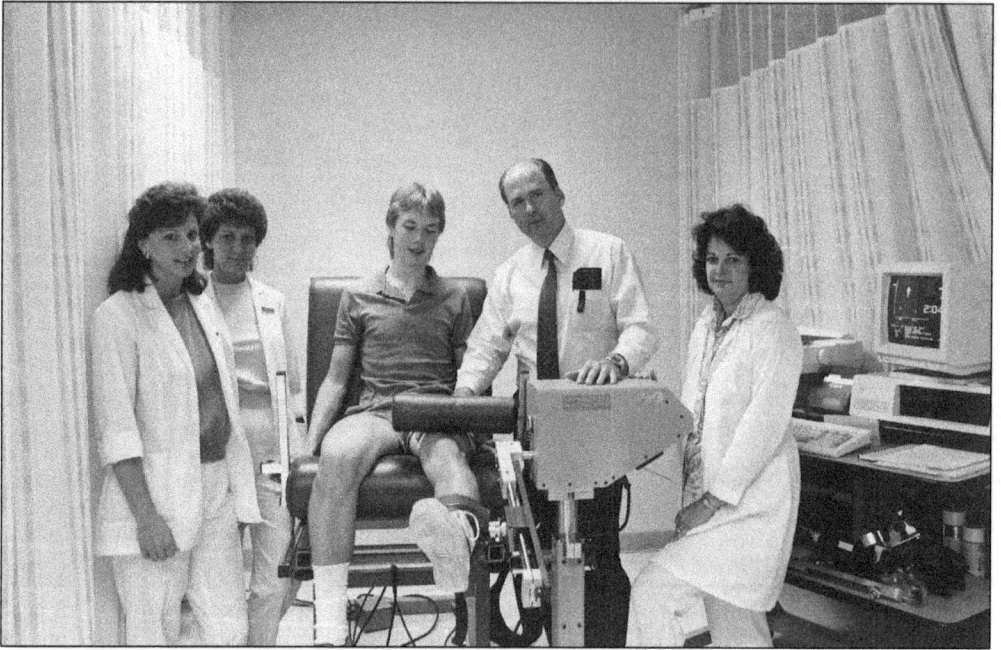

In the early 1980s, therapy at the Elbert Memorial Hospital is shown taking place under the watchful eye of its professional staff. In this photograph are, from left to right, Melanie Almond, Debra Sanders, patient Kevin Brady, orthopedic surgeon Dr. DeWitt Jones, and P. Jo Phelps, head of the physical therapy program. (Courtesy of the *Elberton Star*.)

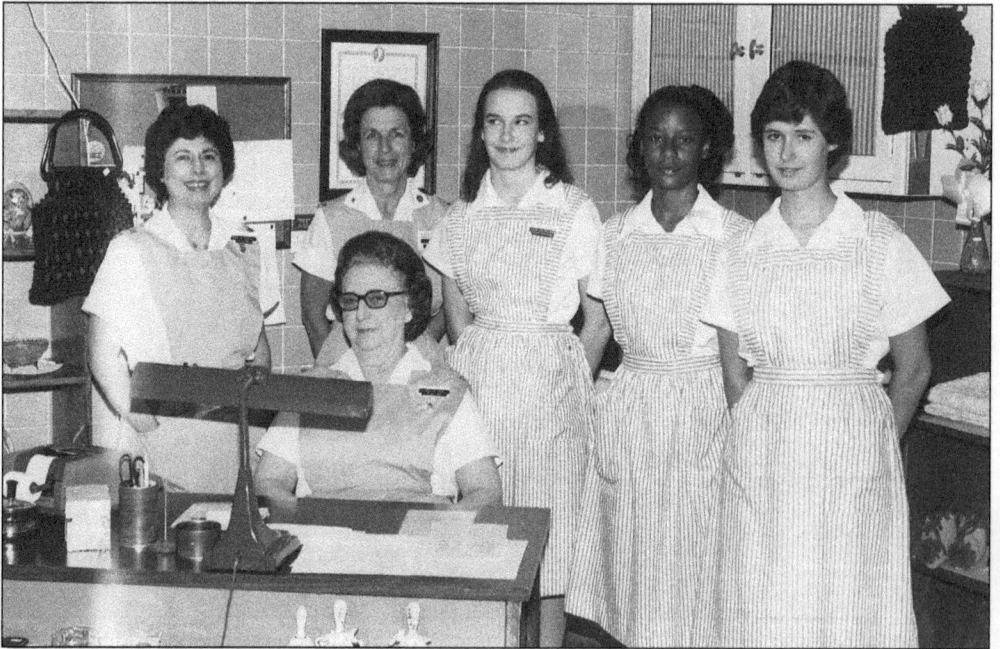

Candy stripers and the auxiliary of the Elbert Memorial Hospital, which was established November 1970, aid the regular hospital staff. They include, from left to right, (first row) Edna Goss; (second row) unidentified, Mary Alice Lee, Carol Ann Seymour, Tammy Hubbard, and Renae Rogers. (Courtesy of the *Elberton Star*.)

Elbert County 4-H Club volunteers and leaders participated in the Volunteer Leader Retreat for the organization at Rock Eagle, Georgia, in 1981. Volunteers and leaders included here are, from left to right, (first row) Stockton Jones, Martha Ivester, David Jones, Sonya Jones, Marie Branan, and Mark Shirley, 4-H representative for Elberton; (second row) Richard Brady, Sandra Brady, Martha Lee Jones, Connie Ivester, Elaine T. Cleveland, and Tom Cleveland. (Courtesy of the *Elberton Star*.)

The waters at the Richard B. Russell Dam and Lake, completed in 1985 and seen here from the visitors' center, have provided an extensive array of opportunities for water sports to the community. (Photograph by the author.)

In March 1987, Pilot Club president Valgene Anderson (left) presents the Handicapped Professional Woman of the Year award for 1986–1987 to Joy Tribble (center), while president-elect Pat Jarvis (right) looks on. (Courtesy of the *Elberton Star*.)

Graniteers Horace Harper, Elbert County commissioner from District 1 (left), and Frank Coggins Jr., longtime leader of the granite industry in the county and winner of the 2010 Elbert County Chamber of Commerce Community Service Award, converse at one of the numerous business-related social events Elberton's graniteers attend. (Courtesy of the *Elberton Star*.)

Gathered to publicize the 7th Annual Granite City Arts and Crafts Festival in 1987 are, from left to right, (first row) Renae Rogers; (second row) Tom Robinson, Sam Cunningham, Steve Howe, Kirby Tyler, Janet Wiley, Dot McDonald, Mary Jean Eaves, and Jane Coleman. (Courtesy of the *Elberton Star*.)

Graniteers George T. and Josephine Oglesby celebrate their 50th wedding anniversary in 1987. George T. Oglesby was the first president of the Elberton Granite Association, Inc., in 1951–1952. (Courtesy of the *Elberton Star*.)

In May 1981, Judge Robert Heard (right), a native of Elberton and descendant of Gov. Stephen Heard, was given the Respect for Law Week Award by the Elberton Optimist Club. Heard served as a state court judge for 24 years as well as both city and county attorney and a member of the state legislature. He was presented the award by Tom Hodges, club chairman for the Law Week Committee. (Courtesy of the Elberton Star.)

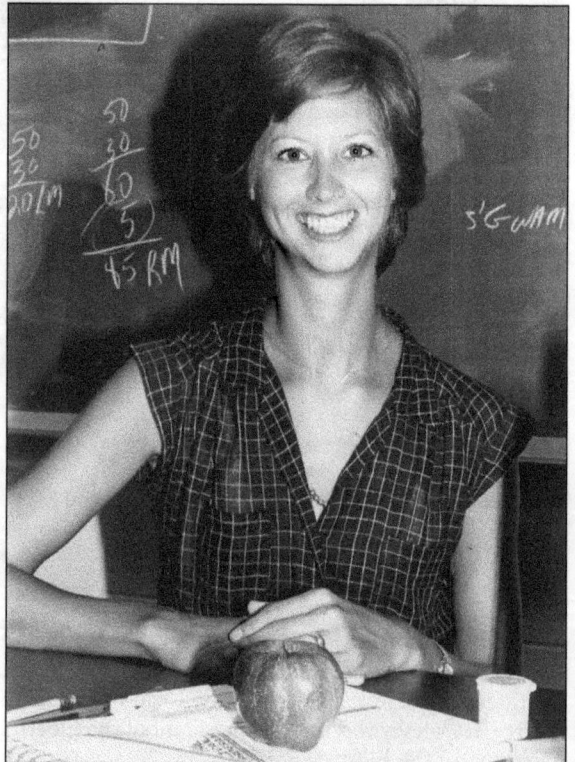

Nancy Bessinger was a teacher of business education at Elbert County Comprehensive High School from 1976 to 2008 and vocational supervisor for the last 10 years of her tenure. Here she smiles for her students, possibly those who presented her with the apple in the foreground. (Courtesy of the Elberton Star.)

Bill Scott, who worked in the granite industry, began teaching granite techniques in the granite lab of Elbert County Comprehensive High School in the early 1980s. He also served as the supervisor of granite projects using Elberton granite at the Vocational Industrial Clubs of America International Skills Olympics, a worldwide granite competition held in Atlanta in 1981. (Courtesy of the *Elberton Star*.)

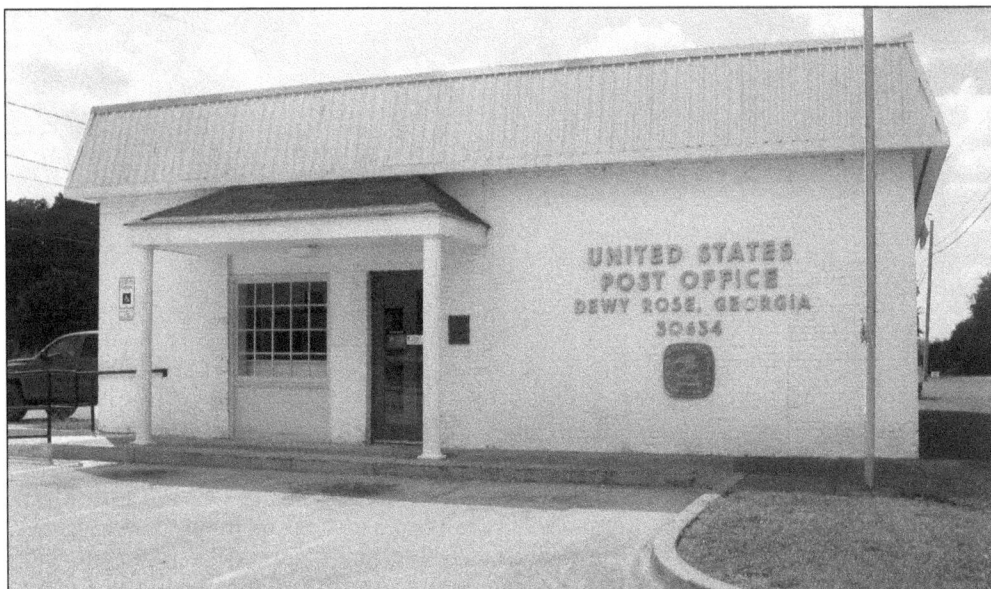

The Dewy Rose Post Office was constructed in 1978 during the administration of Pres. Jimmy Carter. (Photograph by the author.)

In May 1988, Doves Creek Church, on the Athens Highway, celebrated its bicentennial. The church, which was founded through the efforts of the Reverend Dozier Thornton, is here being memorialized by the Reverend Marshall Smith. (Photograph by the author.)

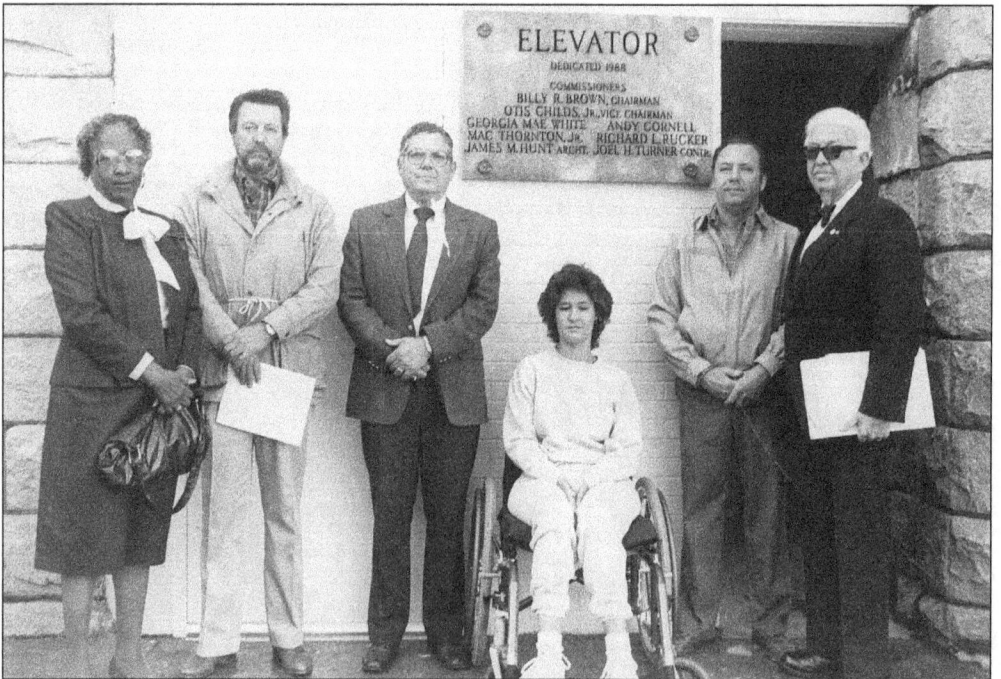

Installation of an elevator at the rear of the Elbert County Courthouse in 1988 was a significant early step in making the public facility accessible to all. On hand to mark the landmark addition are, from left to right, Georgia Mae White, Elbert County commissioner; Joel Turner, contractor; Billy Ray Brown, chairman of the board of commissioners; Renae Rogers Moon; Otis Childs Jr., vice chairman of the Elbert County Board of Commissioners; and James M. Hunt, architect. (Courtesy of the *Elberton Star.*)

Dr. John B. O'Neal served the medical needs of Elbert County for decades, until his death in 1993. In addition to his professional medical interests, Dr. O'Neal also served as a civic leader who led the effort to construct the Elbert County Civic Center. Dr. O'Neal and his wife, Dr. Phyllis O'Neal, who is also deceased, were leaders of the community and were honored for their efforts with many awards during their lifetimes. (Courtesy of the *Elberton Star.*)

Otha E. Thornton Jr. excelled as a member of the Boy Scouts of America in his youth. As an adult, he achieved major success outside Elbert County and, while serving as director of human resources for the White House Communications Agency, was named Native Citizen of 2008 by the Elbert County Chamber of Commerce. (Courtesy of the *Elberton Star.*)

In 1986, officers of the Philomathea Lodge No. 25 of Masons assembled wearing their ceremonial aprons. They are, from left to right, (first row) Clay Ouzts, Wayne Wade, Tim Prince, and Johnny Perry; (second row) Noble Wallace, Ricky Sauls, Joe Johnson, Dan Jones, and Clifford Griggs. (Courtesy of the *Elberton Star*.)

The Rotary Club of Elberton is one of many organizations in the county dedicated to service. Here Pam Smith (left) joins her husband, Larry Smith (beside her), who served as the 1988–1989 Rotary president, in the presentation of a granite nameplate to Bates Thomas (second from right), Rotary district governor, and Mrs. Thomas. (Courtesy of the *Elberton Star*.)

Elbert County Middle School students Laurie Morton (left) and Melinda Wallace (right) visit senior citizen Drew Oglesby. (Courtesy of the *Elberton Star*.)

In 1987, when Luther Burton (right) retired from 25 years of service at the First National Bank, December 15 was declared Luther Burton Day in Elberton by the City of Elberton. His boss, Jack McConnell (left), president of the bank, prepares to cut part of the celebratory cake for Burton. (Courtesy of the *Elberton Star*.)

In October 1982, the new officers for 1982–1983 of the Elbert County Historical Society posed in front of Elberton's Christmas Tree House, home of the society at the time and considered to be the site of the first Christmas tree in Georgia. The officers are, from left to right, corresponding secretary Billy Walker, president Mary Jean Eaves, treasurer Bob Ward, recording secretary Ann Gunter, and vice president Jack McVeigh. (Courtesy of the Elbert County Historical Society.)

The sanctuary of Carlton Grove Church on Petersburg Road has illuminated stained glass windows dedicated to the memory of past church officers, whose names are inscribed at the lower levels. Here, acting head deacon Carl Davis provides a warm welcome to his church. (Photograph by the author.)

Seven

BICENTENNIAL FEVER

In 1990, Elbert County celebrated its two centuries with an elaborate bicentennial program, beginning January 1 and continuing through the end of December; its highlight was a one-month series of special events beginning August 24 and ending September 23. Throughout the year, the *Elberton Star* published articles, including a feature titled the "Bicentennial Minute," a short and concise account of a fragment of county history placed on the front page of each edition. Special publications included a bicentennial cookbook and the *Elbert County Bicentennial Commemorative Historical Book*. Historical preservation had already woven its way into the fabric of modern Elbert County, with the formation, in 1975–1976, of the Elbert County Historical Society. The society acquired a long-term lease from Elbert County on the vacated Seaboard Air Line Depot and, from 1986 to 1989, restored the building for use as the meetinghouse of the society, while also having it placed on the National Register of Historic Places.

Sam Cunningham was general chairman of the bicentennial, and the bicentennial committee inaugurated a month of festive activities in late August. The Seaboard Air Line Depot was selected as the Elbert County bicentennial headquarters. Toward the end of the festivities, the extravaganza was summarized in a succinct headline of the September 19 issue of the *Elberton Star* as "200 Years of Adventure." On August 24, the formal opening ceremony kicking off the two-week period of jam-packed events took place at the old depot. Almost everyone in attendance was in period costume.

Major events held throughout the celebration included a caravan of celebrants to Bowman and Royston, in costume, followed by a promenade and kangaroo court. These events were repeated the following weeks at the Elberton Granite Bowl; in Abbeville and Anderson, South Carolina; and in Washington, Tignall, and Lexington, Georgia. Among many historical activities held during the festival were beard judging contests, tours and programs at historical sites, agricultural promotional events, and old-fashioned field days and bicycle parades. Similar activities led up to the bicentennial pageant on Saturday, September 22, when Iris Anderson, voted "First Lady of the Bicentennial," was crowned, with her court—Diane S. Johnson, first runner-up; Martha Jones; Lula Belle Owens; Dot Gaines; Brenda Floyd; and Bessie Sanders—joining her. On Sunday September 23, the bicentennial time capsule was buried on the Elberton Square.

Gene Anderson, who was in charge of the bicentennial headquarters at the old Seaboard Air Line Depot, home of the Elbert County Historical Society, is seen here speaking at the opening event, in front of the depot on August 24, 1990. (Courtesy of Iris and Gene Anderson.)

The Bowman Community Bicentennial Float features a replica of Bowman's famous well, whose construction and use represent part of the story of 200 years of remarkable Elbert County history, from the early days following the American Revolution to the modern era. (Courtesy of Iris and Gene Anderson.)

At one of many Elbert County bicentennial events held on the square on the western end in front of the Elbert County Courthouse, Gene Anderson (center, left), commander of the bicentennial headquarters, roused the audience. (Courtesy of Iris and Gene Anderson.)

Iris Anderson (seated, right) was named First Lady of the Elbert County bicentennial in 1990. Members of her court, Diane S. Johnson (seated left), first runner-up; standing, from left to right, Martha Jones, Lula Belle Owens, Dot Gaines, Brenda Floyd, and Bessie Sanders, posed with prizes they won in the contest. (Courtesy of the *Elberton Star*.)

The last formal event of the Elbert County bicentennial of 1990 was the burial of a time capsule on Sunday September 23. After the first official shovelsful were thrown in to cover the capsule, all citizens were invited to pitch in and help bury it. In the foreground, Chris Dyal (left) and Matthew Dyal (right), at the event with their parents, Joane and Ernie Dyal, join in and add a shovel of dirt over the time capsule. It will be opened at the next milestone in the county's history. (Courtesy of Joane and Ernie Dyal.)

Eight

PRESENT AND FUTURE

In the early 21st century, historical interest in the story of Elbert County and its heroes from every era and every field is at its apex, and historic preservation joins the field of travel and tourism to make the county an adventure site for travelers and residents alike.

Sports and recreation also remain popular. Leisure activities available throughout the year include tennis at the B. Frank Coggins Sr. Tennis Court Complex of McWilliams Memorial Park, golf at Lake Arrowhead Pointe Golf Course and the Elberton Country Club, and water sports at the Richard B. Russell Park and Beaverdam Marina. Senior citizens have access to a wide range of activities at the senior center of McWilliams Memorial Park. The Bobby Brown State Park is another site.

In spectator sports, games played by the Elbert County Comprehensive High School Blue Devil football teams dominate the fall sports calendar, as the home team proudly plays its games in the majestic Granite Bowl. Elbert County Middle School games, as well as other sports such as basketball, tennis, golf, and track and field, played by various county sports teams, also provide a wide range of opportunities to view these competitive activities by young athletes.

Cultural activities include membership in social and service organizations, such as Pilot Club, Kiwanis Club, and Rotary Club, among others. The Elbert County Historical Society has provided the much needed service of research and preservation of Elbert County history and has featured programs of historical interest at its monthly meetings. Art is showcased in auctions held by the Elbert Memorial Hospital Foundation and in other special exhibitions; and theatrical productions are presented by the Elbert Theatre Foundation, which recovered and renovated the 1940 art deco Elbert Theatre as a community theater.

Notably in the business world, the Elbert County Chamber of Commerce maintains the high standards it has followed throughout its history since its initial organization in 1909 and reorganization in the early 1920s. Finally, a variety of recently opened and well-established restaurants offer good food in atmospheric settings with nostalgic appeal to those interested in the past. A number of specialty shops and stores have been opened in historic buildings as well. Large annual open-air festivals on the public square in early November also draw large numbers of participants.

In recent years, too, Elberton and Elbert County have had opportunities to showcase their historic districts and restored leisure settings by hosting Leadership Georgia, Georgia Historical Preservation groups, and the Georgia Trust for Historic Preservation Ramble. New projects are underway, too; as they come to fruition, Elbert County citizens will rise to meet challenges of preserving their past history and accomplishments and proudly planning for continued growth in the future.

As Elbert County joins many communities nationwide in researching and restoring its past, images of early county heroes appear in a wide variety of settings. The spirit of Samuel Elbert reappeared here in the spirited enactment of the Revolutionary soldier and namesake of Elbert County by the Reverend Jack McVeigh. The reverend presented a skit as Samuel Elbert for the 2007 Georgia Trust Ramble in Elberton and Elbert County. (Photograph by the author.)

Larry Wilson (below, left) served as state registrar for the Georgia Society of the Sons of the American Revolution (SAR) from 1998 to 2004. He also defines the spirit of 18th-century American patriots in this region as he presents the colors with Wilbur Maney (below, right), 2001–2002 president of the Samuel Elbert Chapter of SAR. Wilson's grandson Ryan Turner (center), youth member of the Samuel Elbert Chapter, plays the drums for the event. (Courtesy of Darla and Larry Wilson.)

When assuming the role of Nancy Hart for educational groups, Audrey Hardin, DAR member and retiree, creates a believable scenario with her costume and props and her striking characterization of Hart. With McVeigh, Wilson, and others, she conveys a vivid reminder of the richness of Elbert County heritage. Here she poses with her long gun at the Elbert County Historical Society. (Photograph by the author.)

The new tennis complex at McWilliams Park, honoring B. Frank Coggins Sr., after whom it is named, features a portrait of the late granite leader and a summary of his contributions to the granite industry in Elberton. This includes his leadership role in consolidating the common interests of the graniteers and expanding the role of the Elberton granite industry throughout the world. (Photograph by the author.)

117

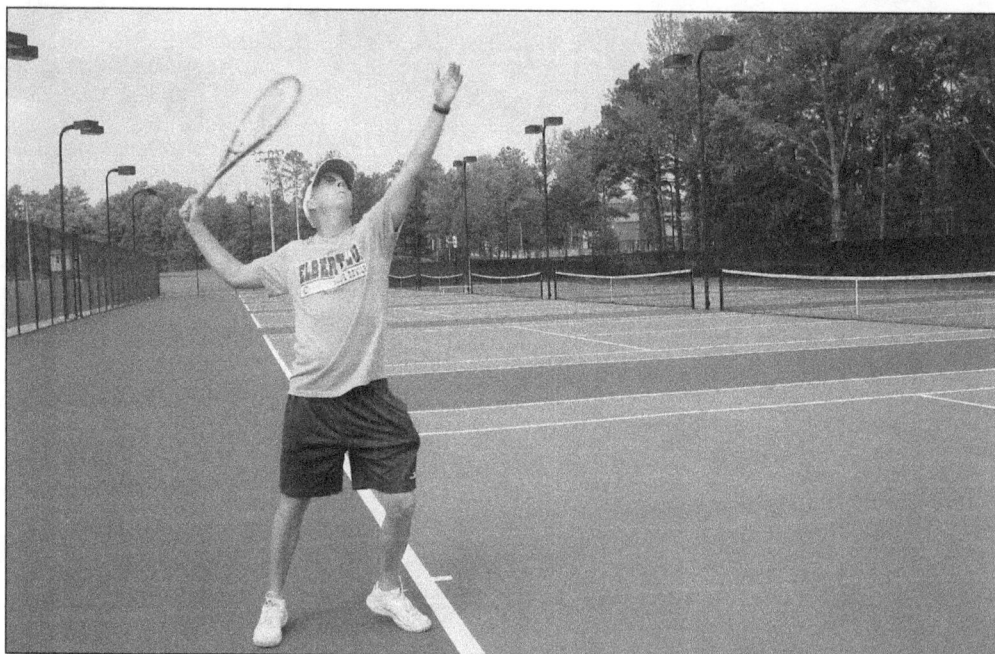

David Bennett, Elbert County art teacher and theater director, plays tennis on the courts of the B. Frank Coggins Sr. Tennis Complex at McWilliams Park. This complex was built in the honor of their father by his children—Frank Coggins Jr., John K. Coggins, and Anne Coggins De Borde. (Photograph by the author.)

A soccer game played by children and adults on an afternoon in December 2009 is an example of one of many sports options available at McWilliams Memorial Park year-round. (Photograph by the author.)

The Elbert County Senior Center opened as part of the McWilliams Memorial Park complex in 2008 and, under the directorship of Rebecca Stephens, has a program of meals for seniors at a reduced fee and a new set of recreational rooms in this brand-new facility. The complex includes rooms for games and other activities for seniors and a future day care center for those with special needs. (Photograph by the author.)

Bob Farmer III poses with the special trophy earned by his father, Bob Farmer Jr., for lettering in five sports. Bob and his wife, Lynda, have donated the trophy to Elbert County Comprehensive High School in memory of his father, who passed away in January 2010. (Photograph by the author.)

Stanley Ayers was a star high school and college athlete and the second and only Elberton High School player, after Bob Farmer Jr., to letter in five sports. He serves as golf pro at Lake Arrowhead Pointe Golf Course, part of Richard B. Russell State Park and named for arrowheads found on the site. Course architect Bob Walker planned the links at Lake Arrowhead so that 10 of its 18 holes have views of the water. (Photograph by the author.)

At one of many events held to celebrate the city of Elberton's bicentennial in 2003, the City of Elberton-Elbert County Historical Society's bicentennial art exhibition featured generic buildings representing early Elberton carved in wood by Alton Almond. Almond's son Wil Hall displays tools his father used for the project. (Photograph by the author.)

Beth McAfee-Hallman (above, left) and Judy Adams (right) serve as guides for tours of Elberton held in September 2007 for participants in Leadership Georgia. (Photograph by the author.)

In 2009, Clark Gaines (right), who achieved great fame in the National Football League, was honored by the Elbert County Chamber of Commerce for a high level of achievement outside his native county. Rik Prince, Elbert County Chamber of Commerce chairman for 2008–2009, is shown with him. (Courtesy of the Elberton Star.)

Members of Tate's Grove Church on Bobby Brown State Park Road prepare for completion of their new church in late summer 2010. Posing after a service in June are, from left to right, (first row) Cameron Frazier; (second row) Susie Burton, church clerk Janie Burton, Josephine Brown, church secretary Imanell Gary, Margie Williams, Stacey Allen, assistant chairman Harold Smith, and Dea. Terry Burton; (third row) Ruby Nell Harris, Lillie Smith, Willie Kate Bone, Fannie Sue Oliver, Addie Lewis, the Reverend Melvine Burton, evangelist Eva Lois Jackson, the Reverend Gregory Allen, Dea. Marion Tate, Willie Floyd, and Sammy Cade. In October 2010, the congregation dedicated the new sanctuary, which is replete with numerous symbols alluding to Christian theology. (Photograph by the author.)

Tena's Jewelry and Gifts is located in the historic old Maxwell House on the western side of the square in Elberton. Shoppers find it to be an authentic part of the revival of old Elberton and its focus on county shoppers. Staff are, from left to right, (first row) owner Sandra Brown, Jennifer Shiflett, and Emily Brown; (second row) Lacey Fincher, Tena Walton, and Debbie McCall. They give every shopper a sense of stepping back in time with their full-service attention. (Photograph by the author.)

Janice Dickerson rings up a sale at Love Unlimited, a store she co-owns and operates with her daughter-in-law Sandy Beggs, in the middle portion of the historic old Gallant Belk building. This store, which features Christian books and objects and also contains a section on local history and culture, has been a mainstay of the redevelopment of shops on the public square in Elberton. (Photograph by the author.)

The Berryman House in Bowman is a popular restaurant which features family-style dining and an inviting and harmonious atmosphere. (Photograph by the author.)

Owners Glenna and Tim Hamilton stand in front of Clifford's Grill, a seafood restaurant, which is part of Beaverdam Marina. (Photograph by the author.)

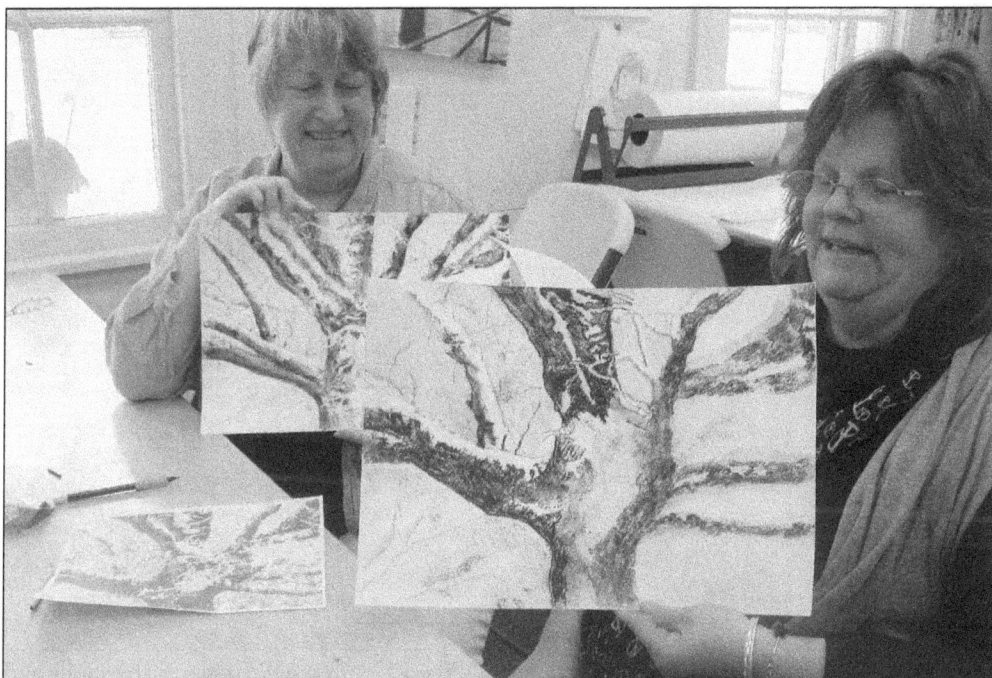

Ann Scott Harvard (left), owner of Blue Frog Arts and a direct descendant of Agnes Scott College founder Agnes Scott, moved to Elberton in 1994. Harvard teaches ceramic painting to classes and individual students and also sponsors art classes taught by other artists at Blue Frog Arts. She often joins the other artists' classes as a student when she is not teaching her own students, and the drawing she holds here is one she produced in a drawing class in 2010. Robbie Parham (right) is also a student in the same drawing class. (Photograph by the author.)

Artist Peggy Sue Kirkland, a student at Blue Frog Arts, stands in front of her ink drawing titled "Honolulu," which is hanging center. Kirkland was accepted into the 16th Annual Hart County Arts Council Exhibition in June 2010, along with drawings by her classmates, Ann Scott Harvard and Robbie Parham. (Courtesy of Peggy Sue Kirkland.)

Jean Smith, a Nebraska native turned resident of Elbert County, sells products she raises and jams and jellies she prepares at a Wednesday morning farmers market on the square in Elberton. (Photograph by the author.)

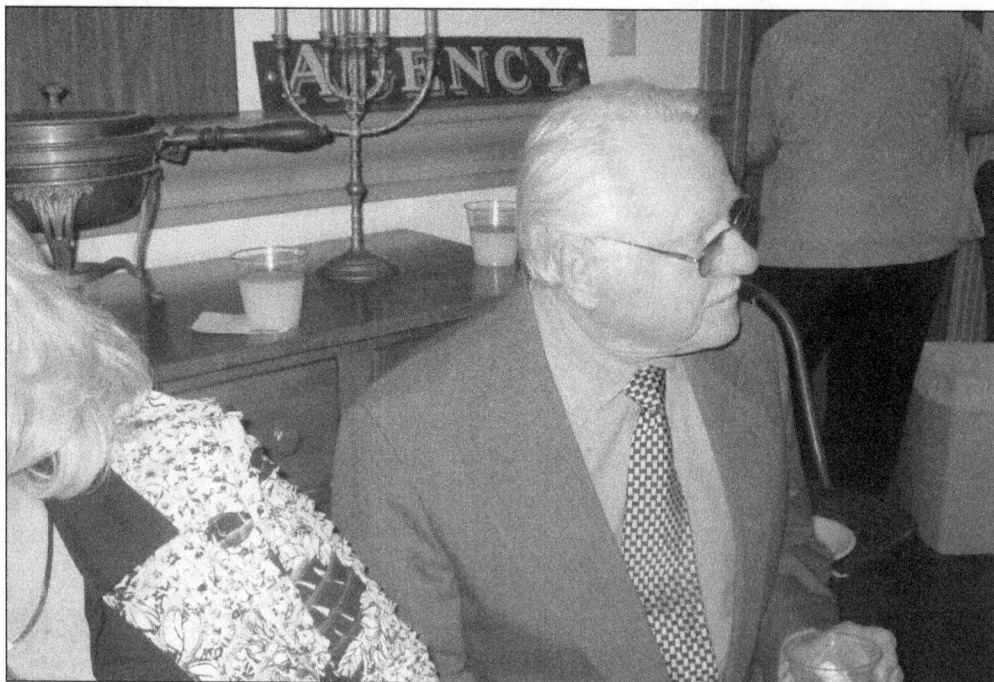

Bill Jones appears here at the May 2010 centennial celebration of the Seaboard Air Line Railroad Depot, which his grandfather, William Oscar Jones, persuaded the railroad to construct in brick. One highlight of the evening was Jones's presentation to the society of a framed antique certificate of railroad shares held by the Jones family. (Photograph by the author.)

The Elbert County Airport-Patz Field was dedicated, upon completion in 1964, to the memory of Florette and Louis Patz, who were killed in an airplane crash in Paris, France, in 1962, at the end of an art tour of the French capital. Some of the improvements made since 1964 include the addition of a beacon in 1979 to aid in navigation and runway extensions in 2010. (Photograph by the author.)

Randy Haralson is the manager of the Elbert County Airport-Patz Field and responsible for all flights into and out of the facility, including those by corporate airplanes. Here he stands next to the new airport sign designed by George Tyler, which includes a real propeller from Tyler's airplane collection. (Photograph by the author.)

Visit us at
arcadiapublishing.com

· ·

www.ingramcontent.com/pod-product-compliance
Lightning Source LLC
Chambersburg PA
CBHW080626110426
42813CB00006B/1614